CAROL CASSADA, TAMSYN BEARD, TAMMY CAMPBELL, TAMMY GODFREY,

Under the Mistletoe Anthology

A Christmas Anthology

WAR GODDESS
PUBLISHING

Contents

I

Care Package For Christmas

By Tammy Campbell

Chapter One

"Hey, Lieutenant. The supply is about ten minutes out. Do you have anything that needs to go back to headquarters?" Sergeant Thomas Caprice asked as he entered my make-shift office.

"Yeah", I replied. Grabbing a sealed envelope, I placed it into a document pouch, zipped it shut, and activated the lock. "Come on. I'll walk up to the landing zone with you."

"I sure hope there's mail on this bird. It's been hard on the men, not getting anything from home for the past few weeks, especially this close to Christmas", Sergeant Caprice said as we walked up to the landing zone.

"Hope so, too. Morale is suffering without it", I responded.

Just as we arrived at the landing zone the familiar 'wip...wip... wip' sound of the helicopter's main rotor signaled its arrival. As soon as it touched down, the pilot killed the engine and he and the co-pilot climbed down to stretch their legs after the long flight from the carrier cruising a hundred or so miles off the coast.

When he saw me, he reached back into the cockpit and retrieved a similar pouch to the one I was holding. Once we exchanged the bags I asked about mail. "Your guys are going to be really happy; I got a ton of it on board", he said.

"Great", I smiled. After exchanging some info on what was happening in the world, I left, leaving the sergeant to organize a work party to unload.

As soon as the first mail bag came off I knew the morale in the camp would skyrocket. As for me I knew there would be nothing from home. I had no family. My father was killed in action when I was fifteen years old and my mother followed six years later, two months before I received my commission. I have a sister, but she was mad at me for joining so she hasn't talked to me in years.

Up until two months ago, I had a fiancé. Then I got the letter. Nine words that crashed my world. 'You're not here. I was lonely. I found someone.' She didn't even sign it.

Returning to my office, which also doubled as my sleeping quarters, I unlocked the bag and retrieved the envelope inside. It contained a single page of orders. To sum it up. 'Remain on station. Continue monitoring the situation. No relief. No going home.

Twenty minutes later I heard the helicopter as it took off heading back to its carrier.

I made my way to the mess tent and remained at the door, out of sight. Inside, Sergeant Caprice and his partner in crime Staff Sergeant James Dean Burton, known as JD to friend and foe alike, were distributing the mail. There were some two dozen large mailbags containing letters, cards, newspapers, magazines, and packages. One particular package was simply addressed 'United States Serviceman, War Zone'. Somehow it found its

4

way here. As was the custom with packages such as this one, each man wrote his name on a slip of paper and placed it into a box. One name would be drawn, and that individual would receive the package.

Sergeant Caprice filled out two slips and held one up for all to see that it had my name before he dropped it into the box. I later discovered that the other slip of paper also had my name on it, but no one saw that one. The sergeant knew, as did everyone else in the unit, about the 'Dear John' letter. Things like that are impossible to keep secret amongst men who live and fight together in the military. He figured that his lieutenant had two shots out of a hundred to win the prize. Little did he or I know at the time, that every man in the outfit had written my name down before placing it into the box.

"Hey, Lieutenant", Sergeant Caprice called out after catching me slipping quietly out of the tent. "you won."

I mumbled my thanks before returning to my office and began opening the package. Packed in Styrofoam peanuts I found two cans of shaving cream and a razor with two eight-packs of blades. Someone had spent some serious money on this gift as I knew that the blades alone ran about twenty bucks a package each. Digging deeper I found a bottle of aftershave and a couple of bottles of shampoo. From the very bottom, I lifted out a Christmas cookie tin. Inside were two dozen homemade Christmas cookies tightly wrapped in aluminum foil. Inside the tin with the cookies was a note that read.

Hello

My name is Penny Campbell and some of my girlfriends at church decided to send Christmas packages to you guys overseas. Not knowing what to send, my dad suggested sending some things that every guy could use. The cookies were my idea.

I cannot begin to tell you how proud and grateful we all are for the sacrifices you have made for our country. It must be very lonely for you to be so far away from family, loved ones, and friends, especially at this time of year.

If you ever feel the need to talk to someone, I would love to hear from you. I have enclosed my address and email at the bottom of this note. I would really like to hear from you. Merry Christmas,

Penny Campbell

I sat there for over an hour eating Christmas cookies and thinking. Finally, I picked up a pad of letter paper and a pen and began to write.

Hello Penny,

My name is Daniel Leonard. I am a lieutenant in the United States Army stationed in Afghanistan. Your father was correct, I can use every one of the items you sent. Thank you so very much for your thoughtfulness and kindness. Words cannot express how much your gifts mean to me.

I have been here a little over four months, and yes, it is lonely. My parents are both gone, and I have a sister, but she won't talk to me until I'm out of the Army. I would very much like to accept your offer to correspond with me. Unfortunately, we have no access to e-mail and depend entirely on snail mail. My mailing address is at the bottom of this note.

I can't tell you where I am exactly or what I am doing for obvious reasons. I can tell you it's always cold with a lot of bad weather

in the winter and hot and dry in the summer. The people here are very unfriendly, and we have to be constantly on guard to protect ourselves.

I have a confession to make. As I sat here writing this letter, I ate every single one of your cookies. They were wonderful and reminded me of happier Christmases a long time ago when I was a little boy. Thank you so very much. Merry Christmas and Happy New Year to you and your family.

    Daniel

Chapter Two

~~~~~~~~~

"Penny, Penny", Susan Campbell called. "Penny, where are you? We have some Christmas cards."

"I am in the library trying to get ahead on my reading for next semester", I replied.

When Susan my mom, walked into the library she found me with my head buried in a college algebra and trig textbook I had open on the table in front of me. "Oh, I don't blame you for trying to get ahead. Mathematics always confused me, too. But it's Christmas Eve, do you think you could put that away for a while?"

"Yeah, you're right. Let's enjoy the holiday and I'll worry about this later", I answered. Closing the book, I watched Mom enter the room with two big handfuls of mail.

Dumping all the mail on the table, she sat and asked me, "Please help me open these cards. Every year we get more and more, and I know some are for you."

"Sure, mom. I really enjoy seeing all these cards and reading everyone's Christmas letters. It's nice to know that you and

Dad have so many friends," I said.

There must have been close to one hundred cards on the table, and we began opening them one-by-one. After about twenty minutes, Mom said, "Here's one addressed to you."

Handing it to me I could tell it was not a Christmas Card. The envelope was too small, it had to be a letter. Looking at the return address, I asked my mother. "Do I know a D. Leonard? I don't even recognize this return address."

"I've not heard that name before. Maybe it's someone you know from school", she answered.

"Maybe," I said, tucking it into my textbook. We continued opening and reading the cards and Christmas letters.

"Are you planning to ride with your father and me to the Christmas Eve Candlelight Service?" Mom asked.

"Of course, you know how much I love that service. When we begin singing 'Silent Night' and everyone's candles are lit it still gives me goosebumps, just like when I was a little girl," I responded.

Later that evening, after returning from church, I was in my room when I picked up my algebra book and found the letter, I had tucked between the pages earlier in the day. I opened it, read it, more than once and I thought...why not answer him?

In my first letter, I wrote about how pretty the town looked all lit up with Christmas lights. How nice the decorations on our house and the neighbors looked. I told him that I was finishing my junior year at the local university, majoring in nursing. I asked him if he had any favorite sports teams, college or professional and if he would like for me to send him articles from the newspaper about them. Nothing too personal, I just tried to be friendly.

Chapter Three

I had just gotten back from a patrol when the supply helicopter arrived at our base. Penny Campbell had written me back. It was a friendly letter filled with stories about Christmas lights and decorations. She told me a little about her studies at her university. I spent a lot of time reading and re-reading that letter.

I wrote back re-calling some of my happy memories of past Christmases before my mother and father died. I told her about my time at the University of Florida, my ROTC classes, and my major in architecture. College athletics was a real interest of mine, but I never could find any information on the Gators.

As time went by the number of letters between us increased in frequency. Sometimes, I received three or four with each mail delivery. Penny and I devised a method, so we would know which letter to read in the proper sequence by writing a number on the back of each envelope.

As the weeks and months went by our letters became more and more personal. We began to reveal some of our most intimate feelings about life and what we looked forward to in the future. In mid-June, just as I finished numbering the back of envelope number 47, the thought struck me that I had fallen in love with a woman I had never met in person. I began another letter expressing to her my deepest feelings. I told her I had fallen in love with her. Before I could mail this letter, I had second thoughts. What if she didn't feel the same way about me? Would this end our relationship? Was I rushing things? I never mailed the letter and left it on my letter pad.

Chapter Four

"Penny, will you be home for dinner tonight?" my mother asked.

"Yes", I replied. I had continued to date after beginning to correspond with Daniel. But seldom went out with the same boy twice. I found them to be shallow and immature. Quite a few had only been interested in one thing and I was not about to let any of them get into my panties.

Later that evening after dinner I went to my room intending to study for an exam, I had the following day. After an hour or so I put away my textbook and notes and, taking a piece of stationary, began a letter to Daniel.

In the first few paragraphs, I wrote about the goings on in school and a few other mundane things. Then I began to write what was really on my mind. I had been thinking about this for the last few weeks and it now seemed to be the time to tell him of my feelings. Having finished the letter, I felt a sense of relief. After addressing the envelope, I sealed the letter inside and put it with my things to be mailed tomorrow on my way to school.

I only hoped Daniel would understand.

Chapter Five

~~~~~~~~~

The third week of August had been a really bad week for me. Two days ago, while out on patrol we were ambushed. Three of my guys were wounded, including JD. They were badly shot up and had to Mede vac out.

But today I received a letter from Penny and things were looking up. Sitting at my desk in my quarters I opened it and began to read. The first few paragraphs were filled with stories about school and such. Toward the bottom of the first page, she became very serious.

Daniel, this is very hard for me to write this to you. I never thought or expected this would happen, but I have fallen in love, and you should know. The man I fell in love with is

On the bottom of the page, I never read the second page. Crumbling the letter, I left it on the desktop as I sat there stunned with tears in my eyes.

Just then Sergeant Caprice burst into my quarters. "Sir, we got trouble coming. One of our patrols spotted a force of fifty or sixty insurgents setting up rocket launchers and mortar positions on the opposite side of the valley. They estimate we have about ninety minutes before they will be ready to attack."

In less than five minutes I had my guys headed out to engage the enemy before they could attack us. The ensuing battle was intense. The last thing I remembered was searing pain in both legs and my head. When I woke up, I was in a hospital bed with a nurse standing over me.

"Welcome back to the land of the living", she said as she recorded my vitals on a clipboard. "The doctor will be in shortly to see you. He'll explain everything to you."

I couldn't answer. I had a tube down my throat and one up my nostril. There were two IV's one in each arm, and I felt like hell.

Sure, enough two minutes later a doctor showed up with a big smile on his face.

"Young man, you don't know how pleased I am to see you awake. It has been touch and go for the last several weeks. I am going to remove the tube from your throat, it's been helping you breathe. The one up your nose and the IV's will have to stay awhile longer."

He spent the next half hour explaining to me the full extent of my injuries, what they had done, and what lay down the road for me. "As soon as we determine that you are stable, we'll put you on a medical flight back to the States and to an Army Hospital for the rest of your recovery", he stated.

The next day they had me sitting up in bed. With the tube out of my throat, I felt somewhat better. At least I could talk a little, although my throat was still sore. That afternoon they removed the tube from my nose but told me the IVs would remain for a couple more days.

Chapter Six

I should never have sent the letter. It was too soon. I acted like a silly little girl in middle school experiencing her first crush. I scared him off. I have very strong feelings for him, but all he wanted was a friend, and now, maybe not even that. It's been weeks, and he hasn't responded. I was so foolish. But…

"Mom, has the mail come?" I called out one afternoon in late September as I arrived home from my last class of the day.

My mom stepped into the room before answering. "Yes, but still no letters for you. Maybe tomorrow, honey, maybe tomorrow." Hugging me tightly she whispered in my ear, "Let's talk to daddy. He has connections and maybe he can find something out. Good or bad you need to know."

My father did have connections. A lot of connections. He was an extremely wealthy man. In addition to his law firm, which was the largest in the entire state, he had made some very wise investments that had made him millions of dollars. Even being able to do all this, he could not control my heart.

He had watched me become more and more depressed and worried over the past several weeks and he had already begun to make some limited inquiries about Lieutenant Daniel Leonard after my mother and I asked for his help.

After dinner that evening I heard him at his desk, picking up the phone and dialing. After a moment I heard, "This is Cary Campbell, may I please talk with the Senator?" After waiting several minutes, I moved close enough to hear the other voice on the line, "Cary it's good to hear your voice. How are Susan and Penny?"

"John", Dad replied, "Susan is fine but Penny has a problem that I hope you can help with." He went on to explain the situation and after exchanging some pleasantries he ended the call.

My Dad told me about his Senator friend many times. They were both Army pilots serving together in an unpopular war. Dad was his wing man and on more than one occasion saved his ass when a MiG got on his tail. Dad was more than a good friend and over the years had never asked for any kind of favors, unlike some of his other supporters.

Chapter Seven

W hen I arrived home that following afternoon I was met at the door by my mother and father. The look on their faces was a mixture of sadness and hope.

"I have something to tell you, Penny", Dad said. "I received some information from John over an hour ago about your Lieutenant Leonard."

I dropped my book bag and ran to my mother's outstretched arms crying, "Oh no, Oh God no! Tell me he's not dead. Please tell me."

"No! No! He is not dead," Dad quickly told me. "Come into the library and sit down so I can tell you everything we know."

"He was wounded, sweetheart. Really, really bad."

We sat and Dad gave me the details of his injuries, "a broken lower leg, a broken arm, some fractured ribs, internal bleeding, and a concussion. A really bad concussion. He was flown to a military hospital in Germany. He was in a coma for almost three weeks and only regained consciousness last week. Yesterday he was flown back to the States and is in the Army Hospital in Pennyland. He is still in critical condition, but he is young and strong and with a lot of hope and prayers he should pull through."

I sat there crying softly and said, "I thought…Daddy, I have got to see him. I have to tell him how much I love him."

"I thought you would", Dad replied. "I have already notified Pete to prep the plane. Your mom and I are going, too. You may need me to run interference to get in to see him since you're not family. We'll leave as soon as we can get to the airport. Your mom has already packed for you. I'll call the Dean at the university and explain why you won't be in class for a while. Now go and get changed."

Six hours later the three of us were in a limo leaving Reagan International headed for Walter Reed National Military Center in Pennyland. While en route Dad made a quick call on his cell phone. "Hello, John. Were here and on the way to the hospital. Should be there in a little over an hour. Thanks for everything."

It was a little after ten at night when the limo driver pulled up to the main entrance. After assisting them in exiting the limo he said, "Mr. Campbell, when you're ready to leave just call my cell and I'll pick you up right here and take you to your hotel."

Walking up to the reception desk my father spoke to a female officer seated behind. "Excuse me. Can you tell me what room Lieutenant Daniel Leonard is in? We wish to see him briefly this evening."

"Well, you can't. Not unless you're family. Visiting hours are over", was the snippy reply. "So, you'll have to leave and come back tomorrow."

The woman failed to notice the Senator and another man in uniform standing to one side and slightly behind her. "Senator, I'll take care of this right now", the man's voice boomed.

"Good evening", he barked. "Do you know who I am?"

Startled she stood, saluted, and stammered, "Yes sir. You are Admiral Shane Anderson the chief executive officer of this hospital."

"This gentleman is a U.S. Senator who chairs the oversight committee for all military hospitals, in addition to other important committees. He also is a close personal friend of the gentleman in front of you along with his family. Now, Mr. Campbell asked you a question and I expect you to provide him with the information he requested. He and his family are to have unlimited access to Lieutenant Leonard anytime, day or night. Do I make myself clear?"

"Aye, aye sir", she replied and quickly sat back at her computer. "He is in room 1801. Just go down the hall to the third bank of elevators. Go to the eighteenth floor. His room is just across from the nurse's station and I do apologize for my rudeness to you."

Admiral Anderson, after shaking hands with John and my father, excused himself to go back to his office before heading home. Mom told me to go up to see Daniel and she, Dad, and John would stay here in the lobby and wait for me.

When I arrived on the eighteenth floor I was met by a nurse, who had been alerted by the receptionist downstairs, and escorted me to Daniel's room.

"He's sleeping now", she said. "He had a bad day today with all the traveling he's done in the past forty-eight hours and was in considerable pain. The doctor has ordered some pain medication in addition to the IVs for fluids and antibiotics."

She pulled a chair over to his bedside and said, "Stay as long as you like. If you need anything, please don't hesitate to ask. I'll be just across the corridor at the nursing station."

As I sat there gazing at his face for the first time, I realized just how handsome he really was. Grasping his hand, I began talking to him in a soft voice.

"Daniel, darling, it's me, Penny. I never imagined our first meeting would take place like this, but I don't care. You're alive and I love you so very, very much."

As I sat there with my thoughts. Time seemed to stand still. I felt a hand on my shoulder and looking up saw my mother's face. "Honey, it's been over two hours. We need to get to the hotel and get some sleep. You will want to be here bright and early when he wakes up tomorrow."

Getting up from my chair I leaned over his bed kissed him lightly on his lips and whispered in his ear. "Good night sweetheart. I'll see you in the morning."

Chapter Eight

I was already awake early in the morning when the night duty nurse stopped in and asked how I felt. My reply was, "I feel great. Much better than yesterday. I slept really well last night but had the strangest dream."

"Do you remember it?" she asked.

"Sure do. My hand was being held, and a woman was telling me how much she loved me, and just before she left she kissed me", I responded. "Strange dream, huh?"

"That was no dream lieutenant. There was a young lady in here last night. She stayed until a little after two this morning before an older woman, her mother I think, came and got her. I saw her kiss you as she was leaving. She told me she would be back this morning as they left. Oh, and by the way here's some mail that finally caught up with you."

She handed me a large envelope containing about a dozen unopened letters and the letter I had been reading before I crumpled it up. I hesitated for a moment before unraveling it.

I re-read the letter and when I got to the part where I stopped and crumpled it I turned to the next page and continued.

Daniel, this is very hard for me to write this to you. I never thought or expected this would happen, but I have fallen in love, and you should know. The man I fell in love with and (second page)

the man I want to spend the rest of my life with is you. Even though I have never seen you in person, I feel as if I have known you all of my life. I have felt this way for a long time now but was afraid to tell you for fear that you would not have the same feelings toward me. Finally, I have the courage to tell you how much I love you.

Please write and, if I am way off base, tell me and I'll...oh, I don't know what I'll do. But please don't keep me in suspense.

Judging from the date on the letter it was mailed over six weeks ago. Even though the circumstances behind me not responding to her letter were beyond my control what must she be thinking? Had she moved on and forgotten about me? Within moments, the good feelings I awoke with were gone, replaced with sadness and a deep depression.

It wasn't fifteen minutes later when a doctor and a tech, pushing a portable X-ray machine, entered my room. He informed me that they were going to remove both my casts and take some pictures of my arm and leg.

After removing the casts, the doctor remarked how dirty and smelly my leg was and after they had taken the x-rays he would have a nurse come in and clean me up. As the doctor left after taking the x-rays he repeated that someone would be in shortly to give me a sponge bath.

As I lay there in my misery with my eyes closed, I sensed someone come into the room. I opened my eyes, and everything was blurred from crying. Blinking away the tears I saw the woman was not wearing a nurse's uniform.

"Daniel, the doctor ordered a sponge bath for you, and I am here to do it", she announced.

I finally was able to focus my eyes and look at her face. Oh, my God! It was Penny. I recognized her from the photograph she had sent me some months past. A nurse entered the room just then with a basin of warm water and some dry towels.

Penny turned and said to her, "Hi. I am Penny Campbell. As you can see from Lieutenant Leonard's chart I have been given unlimited access to him by Admiral Anderson." Taking the basin from her she continued, "I'll give him all the attention he deserves."

I finally regained my voice and stuttered, "When…how…how did you find me?"

"Shsss. All in good time. First, let me clean you up. You know this is one of the first things they taught us how to do in nursing school", she replied.

Using the washcloth from the basin and tube of moisturizing soap she began to gently clean my leg starting at my ankle and gently moving up to my thigh. God! Her hands felt so good, too good I was beginning to have a…reaction. Blushing furiously, I tried to pull the bottom of my hospital gown down without much success. Penny looked at me, smiled, and without saying a word took one of the towels and placed it over my midsection.

Just as she finished and had replaced the sheet and blanket back over me the doctor walked back into the room.

"Good news", he said. "Your arm and leg are healing quite nicely. I am going to replace both of your casts with lightweight fiberglass ones. Can't do much about your ribs other than keeping your chest tightly wrapped. Doctor Lee has ordered an MRI for this afternoon to determine the extent of your internal injuries and a CAT scan of your head. He doesn't anticipate any problems, but he wants to be on the safe side."

Turning to Penny he asked, "Has the nurse been in to get him cleaned up yet?"

"Yes", she answered. "He's squeaky clean now."

"Okay. Someone will be along shortly to move you down to a treatment room, so I can replace the casts", he said to me.

Turning back to Penny he asked, "And who might you be?"

"I am Penny, Penny Campbell", she replied.

"Oh. You're the one…the one with special privileges. Well, you are welcome to remain here or accompany the lieutenant to the treatment room."

"I think I'll go with him. We haven't seen each other in a long, long time and…"

"I understand", he interrupted. "I understand completely", he said winking at me as he left.

Pulling the chair back alongside his bed I sat and held his hand.

"Penny, we have to talk. I am so confused. How did you find me and what are these special privileges you have that everybody seems to know about but me?"

She quickly explained to me how frantic and depressed she had been when my letters stopped coming. She told him how her father had contacted his long-time friend, a U.S. Senator, for help in finding me. Then she began telling me about last night when they arrived at the hospital and how the Senator had contacted Admiral Anderson who arranged for her to have unlimited access. At that point in her story, her mother and father entered the room, and she introduced them to me.

Her mother then went on to explain how distraught her daughter had been in the weeks prior to finding me and how relieved they had been after the Senator had called to disclose my whereabouts.

Her father then stepped up, and shook my good hand, echoing his wife's feelings. "Young man, you have no idea what a relief it is for my daughter, as well as my wife and I, to be here with you today."

We were able to talk for about forty-five minutes before an orderly came with a gurney to move me to a treatment room to have my arm and leg re-cast. Penny's parents said their goodbyes as she accompanied me down the hallway to a nearby treatment room. When the casts were re-applied, she went with me and waited while I underwent the MRI and CAT scans.

Several hours later we were back in my room, and I began explaining why I had initially believed the last letter I read was another 'Dear John' letter and had not discovered the truth until that very morning. When I showed her the letter and she looked at it she easily saw why I was confused. "Oh, Daniel. I am so sorry. Can you ever forgive me?" she pleaded.

"Penny", I replied, "it's me that is begging you to forgive me. I should have known better than to think you would ever do that to me. I'm such an idiot."

I handed her the large envelope from which I had taken her last letter. "Here is my letter pad. I want you to read a letter I wrote to you about three or four months ago."

She opened the envelope, found the pad, extracted a folded sheet of paper, and read the first few lines, Tears formed in her eyes, and she threw both arms around my neck, placed her head on my shoulder, she began sobbing. "You love me...you love me," she repeated over and over again.

"Yes, but I'm fond of my ribs too."

Chapter Nine

O ver the next ten days, Penny and her mom and dad visited me every day. One day her father announced that it was time for them to go home. Before I could say a word, Penny announced she was staying until I was discharged from the hospital.

"Of course," her father said. "I wouldn't have expected anything else. If you need anything, anything at all, just call me, sweetheart."

The weeks flew by with Penny spending every day with me. She was there when I woke up in the morning and didn't leave until I fell asleep in the evening. She went with me and helped with my physical therapy as well as accompanying me to all the tests the doctors put me through to assess my mental condition after recovering from the severe concussion I had experienced.

Finally, in late November, the doctors were ready to discharge me from the hospital. They were concerned about where I would live since I still needed someone to look after me and I had no living relatives.

"He's coming home with me", she told them adamantly. Looking at me she went on, "And there will be no argument from you either."

So, on the Monday before Thanksgiving, I left the hospital. Penny explained to me that we would be flying to her home out west.

"How were you able to get tickets? It's just before the holidays. Aren't all the flights booked?" I asked.

"Oh, we are not flying commercial", she replied. "Dad is flying us home himself."

When we arrived at the airport we went to the private side of the field. Rolling through a security gate we drove onto the apron and up to a business jet. Standing beside the boarding steps stood her father with a big smile on his face.

Turning to Penny with a grin on my face I said, "I don't think you told me everything about your family."

"All in good time", she said kissing me before opening the door of the limo. "All in good time."

Cary Campbell assisted me up of the boarding steps into the cabin of his jet. Penny followed along after seeing that the limo driver safely loaded her luggage and my own into the baggage compartment of the plane.

"We'll be leaving in ten minutes just as soon as my flight plans are cleared, and I get the latest weather report. We should be home in about five and a half hours after wheels up", he informed us. "So, sit back and enjoy the flight. I know I will."

On the flight to Penny's home, she talked at length to me about her family, her father's law firm, and his relationship with the Senator.

"Penny, your father obviously likes me. But I hardly know him. What gives?" I asked.

"Two reasons, Daniel", she answered. "Number one: He loves me and has always trusted my judgment. He wants me to be happy and you make me happy. So, he is happy. Number two: When we were searching for you, he asked the Senator to find out everything there was to know about you. What he learned impressed him very, very much. He told me that you were a man that he could trust to love me and take care of me the rest of my life. Dad told me all about your war record and how you risked your life to save five of your men from certain death when you were ambushed. He respects you and your willingness to sacrifice everything, including your own life, for the men under your command. That's why."

Five and a half hours later we landed at a small private airfield. Taxiing into a hanger Cary shut the engines down and made his way back into the cabin from the cockpit.

"Well, we're home. I love flying, especially in such nice weather", he remarked. "Your mother is already here and ready to take us home."

Sure enough, when the cabin door opened, I saw Susan Campbell standing alongside a large black Lincoln SUV with a big smile on her face. Cary helped me down the boarding steps as I still was somewhat unsteady on my feet after my long hospital stay. As soon as I had both feet safely on the hangar floor, he released my arm and Penny replaced him at my side.

Susan quickly joined us and attached herself to my other arm. "It's wonderful to have you here, Daniel. You look so much better than the last time I saw you."

"Thank you. It's really nice of you to invite me into your home for the holidays", I replied.

Just then Cary joined us after opening the hatch to the luggage compartment and supervising the loading of all of our luggage into the back of the SUV. The two women walked me over to the car and I opened the front passenger side door for Susan and the rear door for Penny. I slid in beside Penny and fastened my shoulder safety belt. Penny sat right next to me fastening the middle seat belt.

"It's about an hour's drive to get to the house. I feel a little tired and I want to snuggle up to you and close my eyes for a bit", she said as Cary drove out the gate from the airfield and onto the highway.

I must have fallen asleep, as well, because the next thing I remembered was waking up when the SUV stopped momentarily to allow an iron gate to open allowing us to proceed up a long driveway. As soon as we stopped an older man came down the steps from the front porch and approached the car.

"Dinner is ready," he informed us as we made our way up the steps to the front door. "I'll see to the luggage after we eat."

Leading the way to the kitchen Cary and the man spoke quietly to one another. Entering the dining room, I saw a large table with six place settings off to one side.

"Oh, where are my manners?" Cary said. "Let me introduce you to Charles Shaneson and his wife Martha. Charles has worked with me for almost forty years now. I was ten years old when he came here, and he has been like a second father to me."

I was somewhat confused. Were Charles and Martha employees or...?

The answer would be soon forthcoming.

"Please sit down", Penny said as she, Martha, and Susan proceeded to put dinner on the table.

Penny turned to me and explained that Charles and Martha were more than employees. "I've known them all my life. They are family. I think of them as my third set of grandparents."

Sitting around the table and listening to the conversation that evening I realized that they were family. I thought to myself that I would have given anything to have had this type of relationship in my life. After dinner, Charles excused himself from the table and left the room. He returned in about fifteen minutes to rejoin us. We continued to talk over dessert and coffee for at least another hour.

"Oh my gosh, look at the time", Penny exclaimed. "You must be exhausted, Daniel. I'll show you your room just as soon as I finish helping Mother and Martha with the dishes."

Standing up from the table, Cary invited Charles and me into his study for a drink while the girls finished cleaning up the kitchen. Floor-to-ceiling bookcases occupied three walls of the room. A large fireplace filled the fourth wall with leather chairs and a sofa arranged in front of the hearth. A large walnut desk and comfortable desk chair completed the room's furnishings.

"Please, sit down while I fix us a drink. Brandy okay with you?" he asked.

While Cary was busy pouring the brandy, Charles walked to the mantle, removed a match, and lit the fire. A few minutes later the ladies rejoined us and Cary poured them each a glass of sherry. The conservation continued with Penny and Martha asking me how I was recovering from my injuries. Penny grasped my arm a little tighter as I explained how my recovery was progressing and how much of a role Penny had played in it. About that time Penny stood and informed them that it was time for me to say goodnight and she would escort me to my room.

The four of them rose and Charles said, "I placed your luggage in your room and took the liberty to unpack for you. Your uniforms are hanging in the closet and the rest of your things are in the dresser. If there is anything you need, please do not hesitate to call upon me."

After kissing her mother, father, Martha, and Charles on the cheek goodnight she walked me out of the study over to the staircase.

"Can you make it up the stairs", she inquired. "Mom and Dad's room is on the second floor", she explained to me. "My room is also on the second floor", she continued. "Your room is on the third floor."

It took me a while to climb the stairs to the third floor, but I made it. She opened the door to a large, spacious room. In addition to the king-size bed, there were two comfortable chairs and a small sofa in front of a fireplace.

Opening a door, Penny showed me the walk-in closet with my uniforms hanging neatly inside. There was a dresser in the closet where my underwear, socks, and t-shirts were folded. Opening another door, she showed me the bathroom where my shaving kit was set out on the marble counter top. The bathroom had a whirlpool tub and a large, tiled shower.

"Oh, did I mention that I'll be moving my room across the hall from you just in case you need anything during the night?"

As she turned to leave, I reached out and grabbed, her turning her around and into my arms. As she tilted her face upwards, I leaned down and kissed her. She threw her arms around my neck and passionately returned the kiss.

"Oh my God, Daniel you have no idea how long I've wanted to do that", she said breaking from my embrace. After several more minutes of increasingly heated kisses, I broke away.

"Sweetheart, I have to stop now, or I won't be able to and I don't want you to break your promise," I whispered as I gently led her to the door. "Remember? The promise you told me about in your letter?"

The following morning as we went down the stairs, she stopped me on the mid-floor landing. Climbing up one step, so we were at eye level, she wrapped her arms around my neck and pulled me close whispering in my ear, "Thank you. I was so ready last night that I forgot all about the promise I made to my mother to save myself until my wedding night. I don't know how I would have felt about myself this morning knowing I broke that promise."

I just hugged her a little tighter before we continued going downstairs for breakfast.

During breakfast, Penny told her mother and father that she was going into town to speak with her advisor about making up what she had missed during her absence from class. She wanted to know if she had time to finish everything before the end of the semester, so she could graduate by Christmas.

Susan said it was fine with her as she needed to do some shopping. I asked to go along as I wanted to buy some civilian clothes, so I didn't have to wear my uniform every day. Cary said he was expecting a conference call later in the morning and would not be able to accompany us.

After breakfast, the girls went back upstairs to get ready to leave. Since my heavy jacket and cover (hat) were in the coat closet downstairs I didn't have to make the climb up to my room again. Cary asked me to join him in the library while I waited for the girls to finish getting ready.

When we were alone, I asked him for his permission to ask Penny to marry me.

He looked at me and placing his hand on my shoulder said, "I cannot give you my permission to marry my daughter. Penny is not my property you do not need my permission to ask her.

She is my daughter and I love her very much. I want her to be happy and you make her happy. With that being said, Susan and I extend to you both our heartfelt blessing. Welcome to the family, son."

I then told him what my plans were in addition to shopping for clothes and asked him to keep it a secret for a few days.

Just then Penny and her mother came into the library announcing they were ready to leave. When we left the front steps, Charles was there in the driveway with the same SUV we had arrived in the night before. This time Susan and Penny sat in the rear seats, and I sat up front while Charles drove.

Several hours later we were back weighed down with all kinds of packages and bags. Cary met us at the door to inquire how we made out with our errands. Penny explained again to her father just what her advisor had told her. It wouldn't be any problem making up what she had missed, and she would be able to graduate on time. Martha relieved me of all my bags of civilian clothes, telling me she would see to put them away in my room for me. Susan and Penny excused themselves to put away what Penny had purchased leaving me alone with Cary.

As soon as they were out of the room Cary gave me a look with a raised eyebrow. "Mission accomplished?"

"Yes sir," I grinned.

Chapter Ten

Thanksgiving Day was a blur. Both sets of Penny's grandparents were there as well as Charles and Martha. I was immediately 'adopted' by both grandmas. Finally, Penny had to rescue me from their clutches.

After dinner, the menfolk adjourned to the living room. This was all new to me, the money and so on. It felt like family, a family I haven't had in a long time.

"Anybody up for some football?" Grandpa Paul asked. "The Cowboys are playing the Giants right now."

Grandpa Paul and Charles were partial to the Giants while Cary and his father, Grandpa Frank, liked the Cowboys. I wasn't about to take sides and said I had a favorite, Kansas City. I just liked watching.

"Very diplomatic answer," Penny called from the hall as she entered the room with the rest of the ladies.

The rest of the day was spent watching TV, talking, laughing, and telling stories, mostly about Penny's early years. I even managed to say a few things about myself to take some of the pressure off Penny. I cannot remember a time when I had so much fun and felt so much a part of a loving family. The next three days flew by and Sunday afternoon the grandparents left for home with promises to return for Christmas.

On Monday, November 28th, a FedEx package arrived for Penny just after lunch. Charles brought it into the library where we are sitting by the fire. As he placed it in front of Penny, Cary glanced at me, and I nodded back with a wink.

When she opened the package she found perfume and assorted cosmetics nestled amongst the Styrofoam peanuts. From the very bottom, she lifted out a Christmas cookie tin. With a puzzled look, she removed the lid from the cookie tin. Opening it she discovered a card and two dozen Christmas cookies. Okay. They weren't homemade but came from a very good German bakery and mistletoe. Opening the card she read:

My Dearest Penny

First, take the mistletoe out of the cookie tin and take it to the person you want to kiss. Then continue to read this letter after.

Penny smiled, got up went over to me with her family in the room, put the mistletoe over my head, and kissed me not long but enough to show she loved me. Then went back to the letter, picked it up and continued to read.

Exactly one year ago today I opened a similar package, and it changed my life forever. Today I am hoping and praying to make that change permanent. Penny, I love you with all my heart and soul. I want to spend the rest of my life loving you.

Will you marry me?

All my love,
  Daniel

What seemed like an eternity to me she didn't say a thing. Looking down into the tin she saw the velvet-covered ring box and removed it from amongst the cookies.

Taking it from her hand I knelt in front of her, opened it and asked, "Will you?"

Crying, almost uncontrollably, she managed to squeak out, "Yes! Oh yes! A thousand times, yes!" She threw herself into my arms almost knocking me over and between kisses she said, "I love you so very much, yes, yes, yes!"

By now Susan was crying just about as much as her daughter and I even detected a tear in Cary's eyes. After everyone had calmed down somewhat Susan asked her daughter when she wanted the wedding to take place.

"I can't think of a better day than Christmas Eve", Penny replied.

"Oh good. That gives us a whole year to plan", Susan said.

"I have to report back to duty on February 27, I have four more months overseas before I'm stateside again.

"We will be married now so I can get information instead of having Dad's friends help me get it," Penny began. "I want all your friends that helped to be invited."

"Are you sure you want to do this fast?" Mom asked again.

"Daniel, what do you want to do?" Dad asked.

"I want to marry her, but I don't want to do it because I'm going back soon," I said.

"I want to marry you now so you will be my husband and you

will never be alone again," Penny said.

"Honey, we can have the wedding when he comes home in June, you always wanted to be a June bride?" Mom said.

"No, No! This Christmas Eve. I don't want to wait. I've been planning my wedding ever since I was a little girl. I know exactly what I want. As a June bride and a Christmas bride. I have it all written down."

Penny kissed me and ran up the stairs to get her book of ideas and her dad sat back and laughed, "My daughter is not letting you go."

"Oh my!" Susan exclaimed, looking at her husband.

Cary shrugged his shoulders and with a huge smile on his face said, "Please try not to max out all the cards and I'll call my brother about the church and have him do the ceremony."

"I can pay for half," I stated.

"Son, let me have this one. I have only one daughter and you're not leaving for a honeymoon until after Christmas. I think New Year will work," Cary said.

"Yes, sir," I said. "I'll do this if Penny can live here until I get back to the States."

"Deal," Cary said.

Susan joined Penny in the dining room to look at Penny's book of what she wanted for the wedding. That left Cary and me in the room alone.

"What's your favorite football team? I know you have one because of how you were watching the bottom of the screen for updates on other games?"

"Kansas City. It's have been my father and my favorite team growing up," I stated.

Cary grabbed his cell and started hitting numbers, "Hi Dale, I need a big favor, Penny wants to get married on Christmas Eve at your church and have you done the ceremony too."

Cary's handed the cell phone to me, "Hello."

"So, you want to marry our Penny?" Dale asked.

"Yes, very much so," I stated. "She is my everything.

"You want to get married this soon?" Dale asked again.

"I want to make Penny happy and if this makes her happy, I will do it," I told him.

"Right answer," Dale said. "Can you hand the phone back to my little brother?

"So, we can, have it?" Daniel asked. "I think that's a good idea. See you tomorrow."

"Excuse me, "Cary said. "I need to talk to Charles."

So, there I was, alone in a very large room, in a very large house because I opened a tin of cookies in a war zone. They were sugar cookies with colorful sprinkles. They have since become my favorite.

THE END

II

Christmas Present Mess-up

By Tammy Godfrey

Chapter One

My name is Professor Ginna Mason, and I'm a professor of history. My husband is also a professor of science. First, I must tell you how I survived Christmas with my family. I'm forty, and my husband and I have decided we want children. I'm not sure why we waited so long, but the long list of excuses always was more important. First, we needed to get married. Then we wanted a house, a car, a boat, and a cottage. Once we had those things, we decided we wanted to spend time enjoying those things.

Before we knew it, Bob had turned forty, and I was close to thirty-eight. We did what all couples do when they want kids. We threw away the condoms and started fucking like bunnies. It was incredible. A year later, we still weren't pregnant, so the parade of visits to the doctors began. The result was simple. We were both fertile, but our timing was off.

I read up on everything I could and decided that taking my temperature every morning and checking how wet I was, was the best solution. After two months, I knew exactly when I was ovulating, exactly when my window of conception was open, but still had no baby.

The next idea I had was to do an ovulation test when needed. The first month I tested almost ten times a day, and I was thankful that the local dollar store sold the tests in three packs. I'm sure the woman behind the counter thought I was crazy, especially since I bought twenty dollars, worth of tests at a time.

November came along, and I was fertile right around Thanksgiving. It was perfect since we stayed inside all weekend and fucked like bunnies. Of course, two weeks later, the evil bitch called 'Aunt Flo' arrived, and we were back to square one.

It wasn't until December 15 that my lovely mother called me to ask me if it was okay and if we were assigned to the small cabin during the holidays. My eyes widened as I suddenly remembered my mom's Christmas get-together, and realized I would be the most fertile right when we were at the cottage with my family. With my mom. My dad. Other family members. I haven't had to hide my amorous activities behind Mom and Dad's back since I was sixteen and going down on the geek who was helping me with my geometry. He wanted to fuck me, but my parents were calling me.

Bob was a good sport about everything, and he knew that he would be required to fuck me three times a day from December twenty-fourth until the twenty-sixth. We were all prepared, or so we thought.

We did it in the morning, packed up, and drove the two hours to the cottage. My parents own a large lot on the lake, and the house is winterized. My mother decided she never saw enough of the family two years ago. It was a great idea to invite everyone for three days and two nights of family fun. This year the house was very crowded. My parents were in their bedroom. My two aunts and uncles were in the two other bedrooms in the main cabin. We were a young couple, so we got the small cabin, a one-room building with windows on all sides and a bed. It was heated, with a lovely fireplace that my dad had put in ten years ago.

The mistletoe was hanging between the front room and the room to the kitchen as it was every year. The tree was by the big window we will be lighting tonight.

The path from the cabin to the cottage was short, so if it wasn't snowing, we could run back and forth without putting on layers of clothing. This was good because I wouldn't say I like the winter and would love my parents' cottage to be somewhere other than Idaho, like Orlando, Florida. Some other place where you can tie a hammock between two palm trees.

There were also four couples: six cousins ranging in age from six to fourteen. They were all sleeping on the floor in the vast living room. My dad didn't measure very well when he built the addition thirty years ago. The living room can fit six couches and at least three televisions. My mom bought these blow-up mattresses on sale, so at least my cousins didn't have to sleep on the old worn couches.

We arrived, and after saying hello to everyone, we decided to do the deed for the second time that day. We went out to the cabin and realized that the heat wasn't turned on. Bob is excellent with fireplaces, so while he did that, I unpacked our things. As I pulled out our toiletries, I realized we would need to run into the main cottage to use the washroom. This was not good, considering there was only one bathroom for fourteen people. In addition, I needed to take a test a few times a day.

"Fuck!"

Bob spun around and looked at me. I was not usually this

high-strung, but this whole baby-making situation drove me crazy. "What's wrong, dear?"

"I forgot my basal thermometer."

"Just borrow one from the bathroom." Bob stepped up to me and ran his hands through my hair. I loved it when he did that because it genuinely made me so aroused.

I nodded and kissed him. He kissed me back, and soon we were under the covers doing it doggie style. I had pillows ready to put under my hips right after we both came, and I winced as he pushed so deep inside me. We used to love it when I was on top, but that was no longer an option. The chance of his fertile cum oozing out of me was too great.

"Remember to make me cum right after you do. It pulls your sperm into my cervix." I had to remind him of these things. When we had sex, he sometimes forgot the primary purpose of fucking three times a day. I wouldn't mind not having to orgasm, but it was a requirement.

"Yes, dear." I couldn't see Bob roll his eyes, but I knew he did. He continued to plow into me and then screamed out as he came. I pushed back hard and moaned as I felt his cum shoot inside me. I imagined every one of his little swimmers moving toward my cervix.

"Make me cum." I hissed those words as I felt Bob's fingers on my clit. He was still deep inside me, and after a few strokes, I was climaxing. Finally, I cried out and collapsed against the bed.

I laid on my back with pillows under my hips for fifteen minutes. During that time, Bob got redressed and decided it was the fireplace's turn to get more wood rather than myself. Once I was allowed to get up, I got dressed and decided to go to the main cabin and spend time with our family.

We walked quickly from our tiny cabin to the main building. It was a short distance, but it was still annoying. We entered and soon were immersed in the festivities. My aunts and mom played cards while my uncles and dad chatted in the sun room. The kids played board games, although my oldest cousin was sitting with her nose in a book. We spoke with everyone, and Christmas Eve dinner would soon be served.

Everyone had to help, including setting up two additional tables to ensure all fourteen of us were sitting together. The tables took up the living room, dining room, and part of the sun room. We ate and chatted, and I was impressed my mother had not yet mentioned anything embarrassing.

As the last dishes were being cleaned, I snuck into the bathroom and did two things. The first was to take one of the ovulation tests. The line was light pink but nowhere near the control line. I knew that meant that I was going to ovulate soon, so there was no question that we would have to have sex again tonight. I also searched through the drawers and found the thermometer. I will need it for tomorrow morning to take my temperature. However, I was worried that using a different one would affect my graph.

I stepped out of the bathroom and was approached by my mother. Now my mother is excellent and everything, but she drives me crazy. I'm an only child, so she tries to spend all her time helping me.

"Ginna! We barely said hello. How are you doing? Are you giving me a grandchild yet?" My mom glanced down and saw that I was holding the thermometer in my hand. My heart was beating fast. "Why do you have the thermometer? Are you feeling all right? Do you need to go to bed?"

"No, mom. I need a thermometer." My voice was low, hoping

no one in the house could hear the conversation. This was not something I wanted other people to attend.

"But why? Are you sick? Tell me."

I rolled my eyes. I could never lie to my mother, as much as I wish I could. I whispered under my breath. "I just need to take my temperature tomorrow morning, that's all."

My mom's facial expression went from concerned to confused. "What?"

"Bob and I are trying to get pregnant, and I have to take my temperature in the morning to see if I have ovulated." I was practically mouthing the words. I could feel my face red, and I was trying to look for Bob or one of my aunts. I needed someone to rescue me from this insanity.

"That's fantastic. Listen, everyone. Bob and Ginna want to have a baby. That's wonderful!" My mother had screeched in my ear and was now screaming at the top of her lungs. I wanted to sink into the floor and die. But instead, she dragged me to Bob and hugged us tightly. "I knew there was a reason I stuck the two of you in the guest cabin. Go have sex. We won't miss you. I want a grandchild next year at this time. So go have a lot of sex."

I looked at Bob, and we couldn't put our boots on fast enough. We practically ran to the cabin and slammed the door shut.

"She drives me crazy." I was so mad, yet I knew we would need to have sex at least once before bed. Bob walked over to put more wood on the fire. That's when I noticed he was staggering a bit.

"How many beers did you have?" I was breathing so hard. I was getting increasingly angry by the minute, and I knew exactly what he would tell me.

"Five. Six," Yeah Bob was drunk. He was a fun drunk, but the problem was that he rarely could get a hard-on when he was intoxicated. I glared at him.

"I tested, and the line was light pink. We need to have sex! Get undressed and lie on the bed."

"I'm so tired. Can we do it tomorrow morning?" Bob was whining but was still undressing. I knew he wasn't going to argue with me. He finally lay back naked on the bed, his cock half-hard.

"Jerk off. I need you hard. I'll even ride you tonight." I was desperate, and finally, as he got somewhat hard, I climbed on top and started riding him. His eyes were closed, so I slapped his chest to keep him awake.

"Don't you dare fall asleep until you cum." I was furious now, but we had to do this. We had to have sex. Otherwise, we might miss that small window of opportunity. Finally, he grunted and came. I barely felt my pussy flood with his cum, but I was satisfied.

"Night." Bob pushed me off him and rolled over. I slid my legs together and lay on my side, fingering myself to an orgasm. Finally, I fell asleep, hoping his sperm had reached my awaiting egg.

I woke up and felt the familiar feeling of Bob's tongue on my pussy. I moaned and spread my legs wider. I didn't open my eyes, deciding to just lay back and enjoy. The room was a little cool, but that meant my hard nipples just got more complicated.

"Morning," I whispered.

Bob looked up and smiled. "Good morning, baby. Do you want your Christmas present now or later?"

"Oh fuck!" I screamed out and accidentally kicked him in the shoulder. "Temperature!" I sat in bed and reached over to fumble for the thermometer I had placed on the night table. I had to take my temperature before anything else, and now the reading was probably going to be wrong.

"Good. I still haven't spiked. You may continue."

"Thanks. So do you want your Christmas present now or later?" Bob was smiling, which meant that whatever he got me was good. I knew that the rest of my family was in the main cabin opening presents and that after we exchanged our presents, we would get dressed and go over and open more gifts. It could be very romantic and sensual if there was a bathroom.

"Later," I leaned over and kissed him softly. It was a sensual kiss, and I reached down to stroke his cock.

"Can you give me a blow job? It's Christmas."

"You know I can't. The saliva will kill the sperm. But I promise the moment I'm pregnant, I will suck your cock for days, weeks, and the whole nine months if you want. But, right now, we need to have sex."

I watched as Bob rolled his eyes but then pushed me gently on my back and guided his cock inside me. He had a great cock. I remember the first time we had sex. It hurt a bit. I was a virgin, so I'm sure that didn't help. But he loved when I told him how great his cock felt inside me. It stretched me, and I felt so complete. He thrust in and out of me. I was close to cumming but needed to wait until he came.

"I think you might like your present now." Bob was grinning, and so I nodded. I watched as he climbed off me and went to the dresser where two gift bags were. One was for him from me. The other was for me from him. The rest of the presents had been brought into the main cabin and were placed under the tree when we arrived. He walked over and put the bag next to me. He slid back inside. I loved the feeling of him inside me for the first time. It always felt so good, so he did that a few times. He would slide his cock out, tap the tip against my clit, then slide it back inside. I whimpered and watched as my juices coated his cock.

I watched as he began to gasp for breath. He gripped my hips and began to pound my pussy. I loved when he went hard, so I just let him fuck me. He grunted and then came inside me. I smiled.

"Here's your present." Bob handed me the gift bag, his cock still deep inside me. I opened it up and then looked confused.

"Hat and mitts?" Inside was a pair of red gloves and a matching hat. I was so confused until I saw the look of complete fear on his face. The only other time I had seen that look was when I was eighteen and thought Bob got me pregnant. I smiled now, considering how ironic it was.

"Fuck!" Bob slid off me, and I felt his fertile cum oozing. I had not yet placed pillows under my hips, but that was not my concern.

That's your mother's present. I mixed them up."

"So?" I was so confused until he explained.

"I bought you a pink rabbit vibrator for Christmas."

"OMG!"

THE END

THE END

III

Love and Priorities/ A Christmas Journey

By Carol Cassada

Chapter One

⊱⊰

"**I**'m not going." Elise Buchanan folded her arms against her chest while glaring at her husband. She never imagined they'd spend the holidays having an argument on Christmas Eve.

"Honey, be reasonable." Caden halted in his packing to look at his wife. "You're always saying the holidays are stressful. So why don't you come with me."

"Oh, yes, that's what I want." Elise rested against the bedroom doorway. "Spending Christmas in a Chicago hotel room alone while you're working."

Five minutes ago, she was humming along to Christmas tunes while making a batch of sugar cookies for his parents' party. While the holidays were usually hectic, Elise was in a jolly mood this year. She was looking forward to some alone time with Caden and surprising him with a special gift. But Elise's excitement was cut short when Caden walked into the kitchen and dropped a bombshell.

"Baby, I've got some news."

Judging by the way he rubbed his hands, Elise sensed it wasn't good news.

"I have to go to Chicago for a business trip."

"When?"

"Tonight." He squinted his eyes as he backed away from the counter afraid of being hit with a pan or rolling pin.

Elise felt the wind being knocked out of her. At first she thought she didn't hear him correctly or he was playing a joke. But Caden wasn't a prankster.

"Caden, you can't go."

"I have to. Mr. Carlson wants me to get a head start on landing the Decadent Chocolates' next campaign."

Elise seethed at the mention of Caden's boss. Caden was one of the top advertising executives at Mr. Carlson's firm. For the past four years, Caden had been breaking his back working on many ad campaigns.

When Elise first met Mr. Carlson, she thought he was a nice man. However, within the past year, her opinion changed. Mr. Carlson was always getting Caden to do his bidding. Whatever Carlson wanted, Caden had to drop everything to please his boss. In May, the couple had to cut their beach trip short because Carlson needed Caden to attend a meeting with a new client.

Elise thought Carlson was taking advantage of Caden's hard work and generosity. She tried to explain her concerns to Caden many times, but he shrugged it off. *Mr. Carlson is a good man. If I do this, I might be in line to become partner, and it'll mean more money for us.* It was unfair for Caden to do all the work, while Mr. Carlson did nothing. Someone with Caden's dedication to work deserved a reward, yet he received nothing. No raise, no promotion, no vacation.

"Tell me, while you're in Chicago working, where is Mr. Carlson?"

"He's in Colorado, skiing with his family." Caden regretted the words the moment they escaped his mouth, knowing it would set Elise off.

"Are you kidding me?" Elise threw her hands in the air.

"Honey, calm down." Caden gripped her shoulders to soothe her.

"No, I will not calm down." She wriggled out of her husband's grasp. "This is ridiculous." She massaged her forehead as she felt a tension headache beginning. "He gets to go on vacation and spend time with his family during the holidays. But you've got to drop everything for a stupid business trip."

"This is one of our biggest clients."

"Why can't the meeting wait until after Christmas?"

"Mr. Carlson says..."

"Mr. Carlson says, Mr. Carlson says," Elise mimicked her husband's voice. "I'm tired of hearing about Mr. Carlson. When are you going to open your eyes and realize he's taking advantage of you?"

"Elise, you're being dramatic." Caden was becoming exasperated by his wife's behavior. She was once supportive of his career, now it was a source of contention for them. Caden was trying to be a good provider for them, and he wished Elise could see that. He knew that if he continued the hard work, he'd move up in the firm.

"I'm just looking out for you. Unlike your boss, I care about you."

Caden glanced up at his wife, annoyed with her criticism. If it wasn't for Mr. Carlson, Caden wouldn't have a high-paying job. They wouldn't have this house and their two cars. He owed his success to his boss.

He finished packing his rolling suitcase as the Uber pulled up. "I have to go." Caden brushed past his wife without another word.

"Caden, please…" Elise followed him downstairs. Judging by his rigid posture, she knew he was upset. "Stay here. Postpone the trip until after the holidays."

"Sorry, but I've got to go." Caden grabbed his coat from the rack, then opened the door. "Goodbye, Elise." He kissed her cheek, but the gesture was devoid of any love.

Elise watched as Caden walked toward the Honda Civic. He hopped in without waving goodbye or looking back in her direction. As the sedan drove away, Elise closed the door. Her lip quivered as tears welled in her eyes.

***

Elise leaned against the door, nervous that if she moved she'd collapse. *He left. He actually left.* She repeated the words to instill what she already knew. Here she was alone on Christmas Eve because Caden prioritized work over her.

She couldn't wrap her head around the change in him. The man who walked out the door wasn't the Caden she fell in love with in high-school. The same Caden who balanced school, working at his dad's hardware store, and dating.

Caden had always been hardworking and loyal. Yet, those traits Elise admired, she now loathed. The past few months Caden showed he was more committed to his job than her.

Mr. Carlson had Caden at his beck and call twenty-four/seven. At first Elise didn't say anything, but as Mr. Carlson's interruptions became frequent; she couldn't stay quiet. When she voiced her concerns, Caden shrugged it off, then promised his diligence would be rewarded. "*Mr. Carlson will give me a promotion. That extra money will come in handy for our future."*

Elise thought about the couple's future. They both wanted children one day, but she didn't want to have a baby Caden wasn't going to be around. That's not the life she wanted. She wanted her loving husband back, but she wondered if she'd already lost him.

***

Caden pressed his forehead against the window as he stared at the gray clouds covering the sun. Pangs of guilt filled him as he thought about Elise. He hated arguing with her and leaving her.

A part of him was tempted to order the driver to turn around, but it was too late. He made his decision, choosing work over his wife...again.

It was becoming a common occurrence in their marriage. He understood why Elise was angry, but he was doing all this for them. Caden wanted to provide a good life for Elise just like his father Jay did for their family.

If anyone asked where Caden got his ambitious personality from, he replied "his dad." As a young boy, Caden was in awe of Jay being his own boss. It took a lot of perseverance in running a business. Jay had a few hiccups early on, but with determination, a friendly demeanor, and creative marketing; he made the hardware store a success.

When Caden started working at the store, he proved he also inherited his dad's charisma and knowledge of tools. He impressed customers and his dad with his commitment to the job. Everyone assumed Caden would take over the family business, but fate had other plans.

In college, a professor noticed Caden's talent for marketing and recommended him for an internship at a local agency. It didn't take long for Caden's work to reach other firms, and Mr. Carlson approached him with a job offer. While the proposition was tempting, Caden had misgivings about leaving the hardware store. But Jay showed he was a supportive father. "I want you to be happy," he told his son.

But was Caden happy?

***

A heartbroken Elise curled on the sofa with a plaid blanket draped over her. It'd been an exhausting day and all she wanted was to sleep away her problems. She kept situating herself to get comfortable, but it was no use.

What she wanted more than anything was her husband here with her. The two of them cuddled together, watching Christmas movies, and eating cookies. But he was on his way to Chicago.

Elise contemplated calling or texting him. She didn't want to spend the holidays fighting. She wanted to tell Caden she loved him and missed him. Yet, as her fingers hovered over the keypad, she lost her courage.

One of them had to make the first move, but it wasn't going to be Elise. At this point, she didn't think anything she said could get Caden to change his mind. It was obvious Mr. Carlson was more important than her.

Caden could be mad all he wanted, but he shouldn't expect an apology. Elise had nothing to feel sorry for. She wasn't going to apologize for caring about Caden's well-being, their marriage, or that his boss was an exploiter.

If anyone should feel guilty it was Caden. He didn't know the hurt he caused Elise every time he canceled plans because of his job. Elise tried to be strong whenever he broke a promise.

But today was the last straw.

The ringing of the phone filled the air. With her eyes closed, Elise reached across the coffee table for her cell. A part of her prayed by some chance Caden was the caller. He'd tell her he was sorry and he was coming home.

"Hello," Elise answered as cheerfully as she could.

"Elise, I'm glad I got in touch with you." Lorraine, her mother-in-law replied. "I was wondering if I could borrow your snowman platter for the party."

In the aftermath of the couple's argument, Elise forgot about the Christmas party. She didn't know how to tell her mother-in-law that Caden wasn't coming. And Elise wasn't in a celebratory mood, so she'd skip the festivities.

Caden's decision to choose work not only affected her, but others as well. Lorraine and Jay loved having the whole family together for Christmas Eve. Everyone would enjoy Lorraine's home cooking, then gather in the living room to open gifts and play games.

Why would Caden choose work over family fun? Maybe he just doesn't care about us anymore. That last thought had Elise breaking down in tears.

"Oh, sweetie. I didn't mean to make you cry," said Lorraine. "I'm sure I've got a platter around here somewhere, I'll use that one."

Unaware that she still had the phone on speaker, Elise cringed at her foolishness.

"It's not that Lorraine," Elise sobbed. She might as well tell her the truth. "Caden left."

"What do you mean he left?"

"He's going to Chicago for a business trip."

"But it's Christmas!" Lorraine shrieked causing Elise to hold the phone away from her ear. "He should have the holidays off."

"I agree. But Mr. Carlson wanted him to meet with a client." From the other end, Elise could hear Lorraine whisper an expletive.

"I swear that old coot is nothing but trouble. He's running poor Caden to death and for what?"

"I tried to explain it to him, but he won't listen."

"He's always had a bit of a stubborn streak." Lorraine briefly paused. "How long ago did he leave?"

Elise was so wound up from the day's events she didn't know what time it was. She glanced at the clock on the wall, it was only three o'clock, but it felt much later.

"He left about forty-five minutes ago."

"Good, maybe we have time to catch him."

"Lorraine, what are you going to do?"

"I'm going to call my son and knock some sense into him."

"I appreciate your help, but…but I don't know if it'll do any good."

"If anybody can set him straight it's me."

Elise faintly smiled. Her mother-in-law was sweet and kind, but could also be stern. From the childhood stories Caden told, Lorraine would put her foot down when he and his sisters got unruly.

"I know you can, but he was in a bad mood when he left. And I—I don't want to create any more tension. I think the best thing is to let him be."

From the other end, Lorraine's heart ached at hearing Elise's dejected tone. Although Lorraine was upset that Caden would be missing Christmas, she knew it was taking a bigger toll on Elise. The poor girl was constantly playing second fiddle to Caden's work, and today served as a reminder.

"Lorraine, I hope you don't mind, but I think I'm going to stay home tonight."

"Are you sure?" She knew Elise was sad, but she hoped her daughter-in-law would join the festivities. "You're welcome to come. We'll still have fun."

"I know we would, but I don't feel like going without Caden."

Lorraine decided not to push the topic any further. "Okay, darling. Whatever you feel like. If you need anything, let us know."

"Thanks Lorraine."

***

Lorraine hung up the phone, then placed her hands on her hips, contemplating her next move. She agreed not to call Caden, but she felt she had to do something. If she didn't then this might be Elise and Caden's last Christmas as a married couple.

"Sweetheart, I need your opinion." Jay entered the kitchen, carrying two hangers. "Which sweater should I wear to the party? This one?" The first sweater had a design of Santa on the beach. "Or this one?" The second sweater featured a reindeer with a red light up nose.

Jay's gaze shifted from the garments to his wife, who had a perturbed expression. "What's wrong?"

"*Your* son's a fool." Lorraine shook her hands in the air.

Jay blew out an exasperated breath. Whenever Lorraine used that phrase it meant one of their kids made her so furious she didn't want to claim them.

"What did Caden do?"

"He's on his way to Chicago for a business trip."

Jay did a double take to make sure he heard her correctly. "He's working? On Christmas?"

63

Lorraine nodded.

"What is that boy thinking?" He draped the sweaters across the back of a chair.

"He's not and that's the problem." Lorraine huffed. "I'm worried."

"Me too." Jay admired his son's dedication to wanting to work. But lately his commitment was going too far. Caden was so focused on being a good employee that he was missing out on other aspects of life. "He's becoming a workaholic. All that labor isn't good for his health…"

"Or his marriage."

Jay arched his eyebrows in response to Lorraine's statement. "Did Elise tell you anything? Is there trouble in paradise?"

"She didn't really come out and say it." Lorraine fiddled with her snowflake charm bracelet. "But you can tell she's unhappy. Frankly, I don't blame her. It's got to be disheartening having your husband neglect you for his job."

If Caden was here right now Jay would probably knock his son upside the head. He didn't know what had gotten into that boy, but that's not how Jay raised him.

"Elise won't take this much longer." Lorraine's heels clicked against the tile floor as she paced. "She's going to hit her breaking point. What if she leaves him? What if they get a divorce? That will crush Caden. Then he'll throw himself deeper into work."

Sensing his wife's panic, Jay enveloped Lorraine in his arms and whispered for her to breathe. She inhaled, then exhaled as her body calmed, but Jay held onto her.

"I'm sorry, honey." She sniffled. "You know I worry about our kids. This ordeal with Caden and Elise has me rattled." Lorraine grasped onto Jay's strong arms. "I know I shouldn't get involved, but I need to help them."

"Sweetie, don't." Jay's reply was met with shock from Lorraine.

"Am I supposed to sit around and do nothing?"

"Yes, because this is a situation for Papa Bear to handle."

***

The airport was bustling with crowds of passengers, some cheerful and some stressful. Caden was among the many travelers who were feeling anxious. With his flight not for another hour, he stood by the window since all the seats were taken.

Why am I doing this? For Mr. Carlson, you dummy. Even Caden had to admit it was stupid agreeing to the business trip on Christmas Eve. He should be home right now helping Elise bake cookies for his parents' party. *The party.* Caden was going to miss out on eggnog, his mom's red velvet cake, and the annual men vs. women game of charades.

Missing out on fun had become a regular occurrence lately. He craved the days when he had downtime. When he and Elise could have dinner, watch a football game, or go on vacation without getting interrupted. Yet,Mr. Carlson put a damper on those plans. Whenever Mr. Carlson called, Caden had to drop everything to please his boss. Today was no exception.

Any other time Caden would have the holidays off, but his boss decided to be a Scrooge.

"Merry Christmas, Caden!" Mr. Carlson cheerily said when Caden answered his call earlier this morning.

"Merry Christmas to you too sir." Immediately Caden became suspicious of his boss calling during holiday break. For a brief moment, Caden got excited at the prospect of getting his wish of a promotion. But then Mr. Carlson dropped the hammer.

"Caden, I hate to do this, but…"

Balling his hand into a fist, Caden regretted his decision to answer the phone.

"I managed to get a meeting with Decadent Chocolates."

"That's great news sir." The company was one of their top clients and Caden was already working extensively on their upcoming Valentine's campaign.

"Yes, but the problem is…the meeting is on the twenty-sixth."

"December twenty-sixth?"

"Yes."

"Wow! I didn't expect it that soon."

"Me either. But that's the only date they had available so I took it." Mr. Carlson paused before speaking again. "Which is why I'm calling."

Here we go. Caden cradled his head in his hand.

"The meeting is in Chicago and I don't know if I'll make it."

"Can you do it via Zoom?"

"We could," Mr. Carlson's tone had a hint of uncertainty. "But it'd be better in person, so they can see your visuals."

It was on short notice, but Caden and Elise didn't have any big plans, opting to stay home. He figured he could make a quick day trip. "I guess I can go. I'll book a light early that morning…"

"Actually, I'd prefer it if you leave right away."

"You mean now?"

"I hate to be a buzzkill, but I think it's better this way. You can arrive early and be well-rested instead of rushing for a flight the day of the meeting."

"Sir, I…"

"Caden, if you do this, I'll be eternally grateful."

His lips disappeared into a line as he fought off a rebuttal.

Instead he did what he always did, comply with his boss' demands.

"Why don't you take your wife with you? It'll be a nice holiday getaway for the two of you. My treat."

Thanks to Mr. Carlson, Caden would be spending Christmas alone in a hotel room miles away from his wife. Caden's mind wandered to the couple's argument. He regretted the way he treated Elise. She had every right to be upset, but Caden was so stressed he wasn't thinking clearly. Then he broke one of their cardinal rules. *Never leave home without saying, "I love you."*

He screwed up big time and he'd have to do something grand to smooth things over with Elise. *Let's hope she'll forgive me.*

Caden's phone buzzed from his coat pocket, he fetched the device and saw his dad as the caller.

"Hello," Caden answered.

"Are you crazy?" Jay huffed into the phone.

"What are talking about?"

"I'm talking about your business trip."

Caden realized Elise probably told his mother. As expected Lorraine would be peeved, and Jay called to lay the guilt trip on him.

"Dad, I know you and mom are upset."

"Yes, we are. But not as bad as Elise."

"Did Elise ask you to call?"

"No. Nobody put us up to this." Jay cleared his throat before continuing. "Son, we're worried about you and Elise."

"Dad..."

"Don't say everything's fine because it's not."

Caden went mum at his father's strict tone.

"You've been ignoring her and canceling plans for work. Elise has been a saint throughout this. But she might be reaching her limit."

The hairs on Caden's neck raised. *Is she leaving me?* He couldn't bear the thought of divorce.

"Did she say…"

"No, she didn't say anything. But there's only so much a woman can take. Your stunt today didn't help matters."

Caden's guilt went from zero to a hundred in the span of a second. *I should've stayed home.*

"Son, I want you to listen and listen carefully." Jay exhaled before beginning his speech. "You've always been a hard worker and want to be a success. We're proud of you. But son, none of that means anything if you don't have anybody to share it with.

Although I had a business to run, I never forgot about my family. I always made time for you, your sisters, and your mother. I arranged my schedule to go in later in the mornings so I could have breakfast and take you to school. Then I took the weekends off so I could attend your Little League games and your sisters' recitals."

Listening to his dad's lecture tugged at Caden's heart. Jay proved he was a real family man, who never put work ahead of his wife and kids. Sadly, the same couldn't be said for Caden. He was missing out on Christmas with Elise because he couldn't stand up to his boss.

Elise is the best thing that happened to Caden and he was taking her for granted. She'd been his biggest cheerleader throughout every milestone in his life. He'd never forget her smile when he announced his new job at the ad agency. Or the tears of joy when they bought their first house.

There was no doubt for Caden that Elise was *the one*. But if he didn't set things right, he'd lose his soulmate.

"Caden, are you still there?"

"Yeah, I'm here." Caden was so wrapped in his thoughts he forgot he was still on the phone. "Dad, I have a favor to ask you."

***

Step one of saving his marriage was underway. Jay was more than happy to comply with Caden's special request. After his talk with his dad, Caden had to make an important call to make.

He dialed Elise's cell number, hoping she'd pick up. But it went to voicemail. *It figures.* Caden believed Elise was either busy or she was ignoring his call. Although he suspected it was the latter.

"Elise, it's me. Baby, I know you're angry and you have every right to be. I was a jerk and I apologize for the way I behaved." He ran a hand through his dark brown hair. "I'm not going to Chicago. I want to spend Christmas with you. Please, don't give up on us. I love you."

With his final words, Caden ended his message.

***

A Hallmark movie played in the background as Elise poured a glass of eggnog. After fixing her drink, she returned to the living room, which was brightened by the colorful Christmas tree.

Elise marveled at the six foot artificial spruce decorated with gold and silver beads, multi-color lights, and eclectic ornaments. Her gaze focused on the mistletoe in the center of the tree, one of their special pieces. Every year, she and Caden had a sweet Christmas morning tradition. They'd sit near the tree to exchange gifts, then after presents the couple kissed under the mistletoe. Taking a sip of eggnog, she glanced at the stacks of gifts, then the mistletoe. *Guess our tradition will have to wait.*

Elise walked to the sofa to watch the rest of the movie. As

she curled her feet, she accidentally knocked her phone to the ground. After Lorraine's call, Elise switched the cell to silent. She didn't feel like talking to anybody. But she decided to check for missed calls and texts.

When she picked up her iPhone, she gasped upon seeing Caden's name. She hit the play button for the message, her heart warmed at hearing his voice. After the first time, she hit replay and listened to the last part.

"He's coming home. We're going to be spending Christmas together."

***

Caden stood outside in the cold as he waited for his dad. By his calculations, Jay should be pulling up any moment. Anticipation was building inside Caden, he wanted to get home to Elise. He'd take her in his arms, beg for forgiveness, and promise to put her as his number one priority.

The phone vibrated in Caden's hand, he flipped it over expecting to see his dad or Elise's name. But Mr. Carlson's moniker flashed on the screen. He shouldn't answer, but he needed to tell Carlson of the change in plans.

"Hello."

"Caden, have you arrived in Chicago yet?"

"No sir."

"No!?" Panic filled Carlson's voice. "What's wrong? A weather delay or mechanical issues?"

"Actually, sir. I'm not leaving tonight." Caden's voice remained firm as he explained his reason. "I'm spending Christmas with my wife and family."

"But we agreed…"

"No, Mr. Carlson…" this was the first time Caden ever interrupted his boss. "You're the one who scheduled the meeting without giving me any notice . Then you ordered me to postpone my holiday break for this business trip. You wouldn't even consider my suggestions of postponing the flight or doing a video chat meeting."

The other line went silent as Carlson took in Caden's assertiveness. "Caden, I apologize. I didn't realize this bothered you so much."

You never take my feelings into consideration.

"Will you still go to Chicago?"

Caden let out an exasperated breath. He just unleashed his pent up frustration and all Carlson was worried about was work.

"No, Mr. Carlson. I won't be going to Chicago because I called Decadent Chocolates and asked if we could do a Zoom presentation. They were more than gracious to accommodate my needs."

From the other end, Mr. Carlson coughed. Caden had been full of surprises today.

"You shouldn't have gone behind my back, Caden. This isn't the type of behavior I expect from an employee, especially one I might consider promoting."

Yeah, like I'm going to get anything from you. "Well, Mr. Carlson, you won't have to worry about that anymore."

"What do you mean?"

"Consider this my two-week notice . I'll help with the Decadent Chocolates campaign, but after that I'm done."

"Caden, you don't mean that."

"Oh, I'm serious." The decision was rash, but Caden believed it would be for the best. He couldn't go on being Mr. Carlson's lackey. He deserved a job where he was treated with respect. "Mr. Carlson, thank you for taking a chance on me. But I think it's time I move on."

***

"Get in," Jay commanded over the rumble of the truck's engine.

Caden tossed his suitcase in the backseat, then hopped in the passenger's side. Once he was settled in, Jay carefully navigated his Dodge Ram away from the curbside and the line of traffic.

"Thanks, dad. I owe you one."

"You want to thank me?" Jay stopped as a line of cars ahead waited to exit. "Work things out with Elise. That's all I ask."

"Don't worry, dad. I've learned my lesson." Caden held his hands next to the vent to warm them. "I just hope she'll forgive me."

Jay detected the apprehension in Caden's voice. "If you two love each other, then you'll be able to work out any issue. Big or small."

Caden smiled in his dad's direction, although Jay was focused on the road. All it took to set him straight was wisdom from dear ole dad.

"So does your boss know you canceled the trip?"

"Yep," Caden signed.

"I take it he was unhappy."

Caden nodded. "Let's just say, I'm out of a job." He didn't go into further detail about quitting, he'd tell Jay about it at a later time.

"I'm sorry, son."

"Well, it might be for the best." He gazed out the window, watching the sky for planes. "After our talk, I did a lot of thinking. I was always busting my butt at the agency and for what?" Caden shrugged. "I haven't gotten a raise or a promotion. I can't even have a vacation."

Jay listened emphatically as he gestured for Caden to continue.

"I was starting to become unhappy, and I didn't realize it until today. If I stayed, the stress would've gotten to me. I'm not going to risk my health, my family or my *marriage* for a job."

The truck's cab became quiet as Jay processed Caden's rant. He gave his son a moment to calm down before asking a pivotal question.

"Have you decided what your next step will be?"

Caden shook his head. "I'm sure I'll find another job. There are plenty of places hiring. Hopefully, I'll find something to suit my needs."

"I've got a solution." Jay glanced at his son, then back at the road. "Come work at the hardware store."

"The store?"

"Yeah, I've been looking for a new manager and you'd be perfect for the position. You know everything about the store. The schedule is less hectic, you'll have more time with Elise."

The incentives piqued Caden's interest. He always wondered what life would've been like if he'd chosen to continue working for his dad. Some of his happiest times were at the store with his father. It'd be awesome working side by side with him again.

***

Twenty minutes later Caden walked into the foyer of his bungalow. The house was quiet, a little too silent in his opinion.

"Elise," he called out, but received no answer.

Panic began to loom as he wondered if Elise left. He walked into the living room, the Christmas tree was lit up so Caden took that as a good sign.

He searched the rest of the lower level, but she wasn't in the dining room or kitchen. A peek into the garage showed Elise's car parked in its usual spot. *She must still be here.* Yet, another thought popped into his mind. What if someone came to pick her up?

Caden then rushed upstairs afraid he'd find Elise's side of the closet cleared out and a goodbye note. But as he neared the top, he saw Elise in the master bedroom. Relief swept through Caden as he caught his breath.

The couple's eyes locked on each other, neither said a word or made a move. Elise sat on the edge of the bed with her legs crossed. Her expression was blank, then her lips curled into a tiny smile.

"Is it safe to come in?"

Elise patted the bed and Caden sat beside her, so close their knees touched.

"I assume you got my message."

She nodded.

Caden exhaled. He knew this was going to be harder than he imagined. "I meant every word I said. I'm sorry, Elise." His voice was filled with sincerity. "I was a jerk. An idiot, a fool...well, you get the picture."

She again nodded.

"I had no right getting mad at you earlier and walking out. Looking back, I think I was madder at myself."

Elise leaned in closer to Caden after hearing his revelation.

"I made myself believe my job was the greatest when in reality it wasn't. The only reason I stayed and obeyed Mr. Carlson's demands is because I wanted to provide a good life for us."

Caden's confessions tugged at her heartstrings. She couldn't believe all that her husband was sacrificing for them.

"But in trying to provide for us, I made things worse. I pushed you away. You didn't deserve that, Elise." Caden felt himself getting choked up. "I don't care if it takes the rest of my life, I promise..."

Elise wrapped her arms around his neck and pulled him in for a kiss. Caden's fingers gently caressed her back as his other hand grasped her hip.

A moment later, Elise pulled away leaving her husband breathless. "You're forgiven."

Still reeling from the kiss, Caden tried to make sure he heard her correctly. "You forgive me?"

"Yes." She playfully squeezed his thigh. "I admit I was irked when you left this morning." She brushed a strand of brown hair behind her ear. "But after what you just told me, I understand things from your perspective. Caden, why didn't you tell me this sooner?"

He shrugged. "As the man of the house...I felt I needed to be strong, put on a brave front."

She shot him a chiding look. "Caden, do you know how dumb that sounds?"

"Yes, it's silly." He rubbed the back of his neck. "For someone so smart, I make a lot of stupid decisions." His wisecrack caused her to faintly giggle.

Elise scooted closer to Caden, who wrapped her in his arm. "Let's be serious for a moment." She relaxed in his embrace. "Caden, I'm your wife and I worry about you. That's why I was mad about Mr. Carlson. He was taking advantage of your kindness."

"You were right all along." Caden's statement surprised Elise. "I should've listened to you instead of turning a blind eye to the situation."

"From now on, we need to discuss our problems." She rested her chin on his shoulder and gazed into his hazel eyes. "If something's wrong, I want you to confide in me. Promise me, Caden."

"I promise." He decided now was the time to tell her about his upcoming career change. "Since we're being honest, there's one other thing I need to share." He rubbed her fingers before clasping her hand. "I quit my job."

Elise's body tensed at the news. "You what?"

"I put in my two weeks' notice."

She couldn't believe what she was hearing. This all seemed like a dream, but this was real. "Caden, are you sure you want to quit?"

"It seems rash, but I've thought carefully about it." He stretched his legs. "If I stayed, nothing would change. Mr. Carlson would continue to take advantage of my kindness. I'd be under more stress; it wouldn't be good for me or you. I deserve a better job where I'll be happy and respected."

"If this is truly what you want, then I'll support you."

"Thanks babe." He kissed her forehead. "Oh, I already have a new job lined up."

"Really? That's great!" So far, this conversation had been filled with one surprise after another. "What's your new job?"

"I'm going to be the manager at dad's hardware store."

Elise beamed with the announcement. "That's wonderful news! I'm so happy for you, baby." She threw herself into Caden's arms, knocking them both on the bed. "This is shaping up to be a good Christmas after all."

"Speaking of, why don't we slip into something more comfortable and *cuddle.*"

"The idea sounds lovely." She kissed him before rising from the bed. "But it'll have to wait until later." She slid on her gold pumps. "We've got a party to attend."

"I'm sure mom and dad won't mind if we skip it."

"No way." Grabbing his arm, she pulled him into a sitting position. "Besides we owe them. I have a feeling they played a role in this."

"They might have."

Although Elise didn't like meddling, this time she was thankful for Lorraine and Jay's help.

"By the way, I need to take the snowman platter to your mom."

***

Caden's peaceful slumber was jolted by Elise shaking him. He yawned before turning on his side to see his wife's cheerful face.

"Up and at 'em." She tousled his bedhead. "It's Christmas. Time to get up and start celebrating."

He glanced at the clock; the red digits showed it was fifteen minutes after eight. "Give me five more minutes."

She cocked her head in his direction. "You can nap later. There are presents to open." She ran her red painted fingernails through his hair. "Plus, there may be a few cinnamon rolls with your name on them."

Caden's droopy eyes popped open. "Well, what are you waiting for? Let's get the festivities started."

Ten minutes later Caden came downstairs where Elise greeted him with a play of cinnamon rolls and his coffee mug. He grabbed a napkin, then one of the pastries.

"These are delicious." He savored the sweet and fluffy treat.

"Hurry up and eat, then we can open gifts."

Caden smiled at his wife's eagerness. She was acting like a little kid, but the magic of the holidays did that to people. Even he was excited, a stark difference from his attitude yesterday.

The couple finished their breakfast, then sat near the tree

to begin the gift giving. Santa and reindeer wrapping paper went flying as they tore into their presents. Within minutes an assortment of clothing, slippers, and cologne and perfume sets were piled on the floor.

Caden finished testing his neck massage pillow as Elise unwrapped her last gift. Opening the mini rectangle box, she saw a silver heart necklace.

"Honey, it's beautiful." She cupped his cheek. Out of all the gifts she received, the best was having Caden here with her. Thanks to a little help from his family, he had a new outlook on life.

"Allow me." Caden picked up the necklace as Elise held up her hair. He hooked the clasps then brushed his knuckles across her back signaling he was done.

Elise looked at the pendant nestled against her flannel pajama top. She traced the *Always and Forever engraving*. The words an endearing reminder of their love.

"It looks more beautiful on you." Caden gave her a peck on the cheek. "Now that we're done with gifts, let's go upstairs. You can model that silk nightgown I got you."

"Actually, I think there might be one more present." She pressed her index finger to her chin.

Caden didn't see any boxes or bags nearby. Then he spotted a square box off to the side. He retrieved the gift, wondering why it was away from the others. The tag had Caden's name on it.

"Elise, what else did you get me?"

"Open it and see."

For some reason, she was anxious to see his reaction. He opened the box to find a teddy bear dressed in a red plaid sweater. Caden was stunned by the gift because he hadn't played with stuffed animals since he was seven. But Elise put a lot of thought into the unique gesture.

"Thanks honey." Caden smiled at her. "This was very thoughtful."

"There's more."

Caden's gaze returned to the box. He was transfixed on the bear and didn't notice the small rectangular item wrapped in tissue paper. Tearing open the gift, his jaw dropped, and his eyes widened at the sight.

The frame held a sonogram photo, and in the corner, Elise taped a handwritten note.

Baby Buchanan

coming in August

"Elise," he was so overwhelmed he couldn't think straight. "You're pregnant?"

She smiled as tears of joy pooled her eyes.

Caden pulled her into his lap, and gently placed a hand on her stomach. He couldn't believe it. They were going to be parents. He was going to be a dad.

They dreamt of this day for a while and the timing was now perfect. With his new job, he'd have plenty of time to dedicate to his wife and child.

"I think this is the best Christmas ever."

"It's been full of surprises." She encircled her arms around his neck. "Merry Christmas, baby. I love you."

"I love you too."

Under the mistletoe, they kissed to celebrate their future. Their lives were changing in big positive ways. Caden wouldn't trade it for anything. He was excited about this new beginning with Elise and their baby.

THE END

IV

What We Should Tell Mom

By Tamsyn Beard

Chapter One

✦

Throughout the Fall semester, I had just one traditional final exam. Besides our completed final scene in Acting 101, I only had final papers and a writing assignment. All the assignments were done and handed in well before I entered that exam. I had already packed for Christmas break at my parent's house, and then I handed in the two blue books filled during the test. I went directly to the car and headed north to my home in Boise, Idaho. As I was approaching Twin Falls, my phone began receiving text messages. Luckily, the Tesla is skilled in reading aloud and transcribing text. I had the freedom to reply to Chloe without needing to stop and pull over.

Chloe: How did your exam go?

   Chloe: My first is this afternoon, and it should be effortless, which has me worried.

   Chloe: LOL

   Me: Mine was more complicated than I thought. But I still crushed it, I guess.

Chloe: Good

Then, a half hour later...

Chloe: Got all your shopping done for your family?

Me: Yep. Thanks to you two. Dad and I have our trip starting Wednesday.

Chloe: Going to kill some poor woodland creatures with your big, bad gun?

Me: It is mostly fishing.

Chloe: Don't drown.

Me: Let's hope.

Chloe: I must get on the road will text or call when I get to my Grandparents house.

Me: I'll miss you.

Chloe: Don't find another girlfriend while you're there.

Me: Trust me, I won't.

Not long after my conversation with Chloe, the phone started ringing. It was Noel.

Our conversation lasted a while. Additionally, she inquired about my exam. Then complained that she had a problem at work. Something unexpected happened that will keep her extremely busy during the entire holiday season. Noel wouldn't be able to go home this year.

"What the hell do we have judges for?" she complained. if not to issue continuances over the holidays. Lawyers can join the firm's Christmas party instead of being stuck in their offices."

"I confidently reassured everyone that the Mighty Noel would conquer her paperwork and join her colleagues for wine at the Christmas party," I added teasingly. "Just don't get too collegian with any coworkers."

84

"Don't worry, darling," Noel replied softly. "What about your parents, like over the Christmas season?"

"My mother was typically fussing over how 'tired' I looked. Demanding to know why I hadn't brought any laundry for her to do. Asking for details of how the semester has gone. She also told me she had planned dinner early, so I could go out later and see old friends. I told her to stop fussing—I was getting plenty of sleep; I was a grown-ass man and could do my laundry without bringing it home to Mom. Although I was not behind on the rest, I was tired and wanted to hang out with her, Dad, and my sister. Maybe we could play some card games."

"Have fun. I'll be calling to check in," Noel said.

"Remember the fishing trip starts Wednesday," I stated.

"I have it marked on my calendar. Have a fun trip, love," Noel said.

Chapter Two

꧁ৎ꧂

The following day, I chauffeured my younger sister, braved Christmas shopping, and ran errands for Mom. Darcy's car was left at school when she chose to fly home, so someone had to deal with it driving her around town. Darcy, a freshman at Ole Miss, is remarkably pleasant and enjoyable to talk to as a little sister. A single afternoon of undivided attention was precisely what I needed.

I spent the afternoon questioning her about the college guys. I knew they were all over her, like a fly on rice, all the while carefully lying through my teeth about my love life. I was convinced that Darcy was getting laid, possibly regularly, and began with astounding hypocrisy. So now I must plot an unannounced visit to Oxford to put the fear of God into a few selected dudes.

I made the visit and discovered that there was only one guy. He had an astonishingly low level of maturity for a sophomore, and he and Darcy were a couple for two months until she eventually ended the relationship. He was a complete asshole.

I like most of the guys my sister brought home, but not him.

Upon our return to the house, my sister and I joined everyone for a meal. Mom seemed surprised that her children wanted to spend time with her, and she asked us, well me, twice if we wanted to do something on our own with friends instead. Following dinner, Darcy ended up catching a movie with an old pal. My happiness perplexed Mom about preparing for our yearly trip and spending time with her and Dad.

"Are you trying to get rid of me, Mom?" I complained. "We're leaving early tomorrow, and I don't want to sleep the entire ride. It would be particularly problematic for the sections where I'm driving."

"Late nights never stopped you before now," she just replied.

"I'm an old man now. I need my rest," I sparked. "Seriously, Mom. Chuck is doing Christmas in the mountains this year with his family, and Pete has to work tonight."

When I told her I was going out to get a burger, she finally left me alone. I packed and watched Netflix when I got home.

Chapter Three

The day after, my father and I started our journey. There's an accessible drive west of me that takes you to a lot of friendly wildernesses. Before Christmas, he and I spent three or four days relaxing in the woods, away from the women in our family. Despite our small number of two, it seemed like we were outnumbered by about four to one. My parents named me Steven after my Dad, but they never called me Junior.

My dad is extremely successful. Despite starting off with my dad, but they never called me Junior even though I have the junior at the end of my name with an advantage, he has achieved greater success than others in his situation. The long hours and frequent travel made him a distant figure most of the time. Despite everything, he always gave his full attention to his family when he was with them. The times he designated for us were firm and unchangeable.

He made it to very few of Darcy's or my softball games to golf tournaments. Without fail, whenever he mentioned his arrival, he remained present for the duration. Trying not to jeer the refs (and failing) and flirting with our teammate's moms in the best tradition of youth sports parenting. For him, there was none of that last-second ghosting you see in the movies. The negligent father opts for a last-minute meeting, demonstrating to the child that they are not his main concern. That was not my Dad.

Dad always made sure to allocate specific times for each of us every year, and those plans never failed. Twice a year, every year, he and my mom would travel outside the country. Generally, not within the continent. If they were lucky enough to find the internet, his phone and laptop were always packed away in the suitcase. I honestly can't understand why Darcy and I don't have more siblings. My parents' intense attraction to each other serves as inspiration as you grow older. Before school starts, he annually takes Darcy to New York so she can shop without Mom's interference. Dad enjoys drinking unique cocktails at Manhattan bars late into the night without Mom's interruption.

My block of time happened just before Christmas. Four days. In the woods. We took two small tents. Dad had a pop-up trailer that he kept for years. Bring coolers, beer, camp chairs, and other essentials for a comfortable campsite that lives up to its name. Our fly rods were securely stored in the cabin of Dad's beat-up old F-150, which he used for this trip and to occasionally bother my mother. On the rack behind us was my vintage thirty-six with the brand-new scope I had bought myself for my birthday and Dad's black rifle. Although the trip was focused on fishing, we reserved the last day for hunting wild boar. The presence of feral swine is becoming a dangerous problem for farmers, ranchers, gardeners, and small dog owners. It's the reason why they are always in season. I've never killed anything except fish and insects that I didn't eat, it is fortunate that game pork can be tasty if you know how to cook it.

Penny Courtney, I had been lifelong friend but when she turned seventeen it was like the Boob Fairy brought an eighteen-wheeler to my tomboy friend's house, and it made me see her differently. Sadly, her perception of me stayed unchanged indefinitely.

"This year," Dad said, "even I noticed that you didn't go hound-dogging as soon as you got home. Your mother was thrilled with how you tactfully disregarded all her reminders about seeing Penny. What the fuck gives?"

My father refrains from swearing in the presence of women, children, or business acquaintances. When he started swearing around me, it was one of the most incredible moments in my life. It had meant I was a man.

Dad also never swore unless he was livid, or more often when he was having fun so that F-bomb meant I had a problem. Without it, I might have gone with vague reassurances of 'nothing serious,' etc. But now I knew he was amused, which meant he would dig and keep digging.

I fervently prayed for the damned fish to appear. The fuckers did not.

"It's complicated," I tried. I attempted to find some distracting fish by changing where I cast my fly, but it was in vain. Despite that, there might be a couple around. It seemed like they had all consumed a substantial Danish for breakfast and had no appetite. I noticed that if we don't find fish, we'll have to settle for a canned food dinner.

Dad responded dryly with an "Uh-huh," dismissing my hunger concerns. "So, what is the complication? Are you once again in an unrequited love scenario?"

"It is not unrequited! I couldn't control myself and snapped."
Damn.

"Nice!" laughed my father. "If you're constantly getting
'requited', what's the complication?"

I replied with complications, hoping to bring an end to the
conversation and avoid any further response.

"Ah yes," Dad intoned sagely, "The Complications often
complicate matters." The fly flicked across the water. The
bastard let the silence extend just long enough for me to hope
he would let things drop. I should have known better.

"You know," he suddenly said, "the reason humans keep
elderly people like me is to provide wisdom and advice. To help
by passing on our own experiences with these complications."

I laughed, confident that you haven't had to handle this
complication. "I know you never had to deal with this problem."

"Oh ho!" laughed Dad loudly. The noise indicated a potential
delay of 30 minutes before the fish would be likely to bite. "Now
you have me curious."

"Dad, I have always appreciated your support and the way you
have always been there for me when I asked for advice," I said.
"You've never been this insistent on giving it before. What's
your freaking deal?"

Dad shot me a glance and grinned. "I'm a fifty-nine-year-old
man who has been happily married to your mother for most
of my adult life. "He shrugged when the chance to experience
life through his son or any guy in a new relationship came
along." The presence of complications adds to the greatness of
the story."

"Jesus."

"So, what is the problem you are dealing with? Wait."

my father interrupted himself. "Is she a black girl?" He misinterpreted the way my eyes widened. "I'm disappointed, Steven. You know your mother would not have a problem with any girl of any color as long as she loves you."

"Dad!" I interrupted, scaring the fish again with my volume. "I know Mom wouldn't have a problem! Shit! If I were dating a black girl, Grampy Dan could go fuck himself."

"Fuckin-A," replied my father, who was not a great fan of his father-in-law. "But I still don't see the problem. So, after Christmas, drive back to the college, collect the girl, and bring her back for New Year's."

I looked at him, shocked.

"If there's a problem, your mom is the one who fixes it." My father encouraged me to let her give it a shot at helping if manly advice couldn't solve my problem.

"Dad, if I brought two women back home for New Year's, Mom would have a fucking aneurysm," I exclaimed.

As I mentioned previously, my mouth tends to speak before my brain thinks. There are occasions when I am unable to speak and my mouth freezes. This was a situation where the latter option would have been more advantageous. Much better.

My father stared at me. In the depths of my thoughts, I reveled in leaving my father speechless for the first time in years. I was kicking myself out in the front of my mind. Hard.

"There are two girls," Dad said slowly at last. "Two?"

"Two women. Yes," I ground out between clenched teeth. "Mom would have an aneurysm."

My father looked at the sky with a slight smile and rocked his head back and forth. "I don't know, Steven. Your mom might handle that better than you think."

Wait. What? What the... What the actual fuck? My mind

screamed. If only by implication, what did I learn about my mom? It occurred to me that Dad's concern about Mom's freak out might disrupt his interrogation of me. I abandoned the idea when I realized I would be giving a PowerPoint presentation to my parents instead. Diagrams show how I'd fucked Chloe in a restaurant bathroom the prior Friday. I found out what made my father think my mom would be fine with me dating two girls simultaneously.

In the midst of my panicked mental turmoil, my father remained silent momentarily. "Um…" he said carefully. At least someone besides me had decided to be careful with his words. "Are you dating two girls simultaneously, or are you, um… more than just dating them?"

I stared at him. Glared. Despite my determination not to reply, my silence did the talking.

My father sighed and reeled in his line. "We should move up to the next bend. There may be something to catch down there." A change of venue sounded good to me. Any fish in a new spot would not have been scared off by all the hollering.

As we walked upstream, Dad sucked at his teeth. "Um, you know how likely this will end poorly… for all three of you." He paused. "But especially for you?" We trudged on, and I did not answer. "Look," he went on while we struggled through a thicket, "one of them will find out eventually." They always…."

"Not my problem, Dad," I interrupted shortly.

"It will be," he insisted. "You're smart, boy. God knows you are smart. But even the smart ones get caught. Do they know each other?"

I snorted. "Oh yeah. But…."

"Christ, you are fucked." My father was pissing me off. The scrub, which had more of its share of thorns than was strictly reasonable, was pissing me off more.

"They know about each other, Dad," I growled.

My father spun around to look at me when I said that. In doing so, he let go of a branch, which whipped back and spiked him reasonably effectively. I moved to help disentangle him and impaled myself for my sins. We were laughing, and both only a little in pain, when we finally extracted ourselves from the fucking thorns. From there, we waded back into the river and saw that we had found a better-looking location.

In silence, we began casting once more, while I sensed Dad brewing beside me.

"Let me make sure I understand this correctly," he resumed. "There are two women. They know each other. They are both aware that you are fucking the other one at the same time?" His eyebrows were higher than I'd ever seen them.

"Yes," I sighed. Still, feeling extremely humiliated by this exchange. I had to admit that it was immensely God-damned satisfying to have my father on his heels like this. I grinned at myself, primarily when he uttered the phrase "at the same time."

Unfortunately, my father might have been off balance, but he is never anything but observant. It's why I'm such a rules-following, responsible guy. I never got away with one damned thing around him growing up.

And I didn't get away with that little chuckle to myself, either.

His raised eyebrows snapped into a furrow and his eyes narrowed. "Wait, a second. You smiled when I said, at the same time. "Are you having threesomes?!?"

"Yes," I sighed. I was now feeling mortified by the conversation.

His shout scared away any possibility of eating fresh fish that night. His voice must have reached every fish in the entire river.

I bet on fish in Asheville aquariums, heard him.

I couldn't hold back and whispered in a choked voice that they have an aversion to using that term.

My father stared at me. Then he tossed his rod onto a nearby rock and made his way towards me. When he got to me, he stuck out his hand. "Well, put 'er God-damned there," he said with a grin and a gleam in his eye. I bemusedly shook his hand. "I have never met any guy who ever came close to a threesome!" he exclaimed. "Well, except for... Anyway."

Do. Not. Pursue. That. Interrupted. Remark.

"My son pulls it off," he went on. I swear the sonofabitch was proud of me!

He burst into laughter. Hard. He had his hands on his knees while bending over. He was laughing with great intensity. When he finally caught his breath, he turned his attention back to me. "Don't get me wrong, I still think you are fucked in the long run, but you can get away with your balls still attached instead of hanging from their rear view mirrors."

"Yeah," I said, suddenly pensive. My father sensed it and settled down on a vast rock, inviting me to sit down too. The fishing was forgotten.

"I'm joking, you know," he said, arm around me, something he didn't do that often.

I said "Yeah" again, this time with a sigh. "From the very beginning, I've known that I am performing the greatest balancing act in the history of male-female relationships. I'm constantly terrified."

"Good," said my father. "You might get it to last for a while that way." He shut up for a bit. But I felt him fidgeting. "Look," he burst out at last. "This is so wrong, but I'm dying of curiosity. For the duration of this trip, I am not your father. I need to ask questions."

"Dad!"

"My name is Steven, Steven."

"I'm sorry, Steven," I said sweetly. "Have you lost your God-damned fucking mind?" I added it at the top of my lungs.

My father looked at me blandly, then asked calmly, "Are they hot? Is at least one of them hot? I imagine they must be equally attractive, or it would never even start. Am I right?" Christ, was my father babbling? Did I babble because of genetics?

To shut Dad up, I said, "They are both out of my league."

"Really?" My father asked skeptically. "Your mother and I produced a couple of beautiful kids, you know."

"I never knew awesome could come in such different forms," I sighed before I could help myself.

My father laughed to himself with unseemly glee. Then he sobered. "Damn! Now I am the one in trouble."

"Huh?" I asked.

"I have an assignment, Steven! I am to return with the straight poop on this girl of yours. I cannot come back with a story that you are having three-way sex with supermodels!"

"I should fucking hope not!" I said swiftly. But I was secretly thrilled at the turn this conversation had just taken. Dad was terrible enough, but I supposed I could deal with him, especially if he was surprisingly enthusiastic. Mom would be Hell on Earth.

But since I was safe, I might as well tease the old man a little.

"To be fair," I drawled. "It is mostly not threesomes. Usually, it is just the night with one or the other."

"How about when you're gone, like now, do they...keep each other company?"

"No comment."

We ended up catching just one fish during the whole day. One. True, it was beautiful, but dinner would still have too many packaged ingredients for a good camping trip. Oh well.

When we did straggle back into camp, scratched up and happy, though mostly fish-less, I set to my usual task of making the fire. But, first, Dad cleaned the fish, a job that was unfairly easy that night. He finished quickly and then walked over to me.

"Here," he said, snapping his fingers. "Let me finish getting the fire started. Then, you go drag your phone out of the truck and show me some pictures."

Whoa.

Phones were never opened on camping trips. So, this was a historic moment.

And no.

No way he was getting pictures. I was not letting him see either one of them. Especially Noel. For a twenty-three-year-old, it would require some epic preparation to prepare your parents for revealing your twenty-five-year-old smoke show of a girlfriend. I was not good enough at CPR to let my father in on that secret, not out here in the wilderness.

Besides, neither of them was any of my parent's God-damned business.

"Sorry, Dad," I said with elaborately insincere anguish. "I've told you too damned much already. Your son is keeping the exact details of his goddesses to himself."

The sonofabitch dropped the subject. I love my father.

The rest of the trip was routine. We caught so many fish the next day we tossed most back, keeping just enough to eat for that night and the next.

The day we finally left; we did not get on the road home until very late on our last full day in the woods. We had set our rods aside for rifles, and each got a boar. That meant we had to take an extended break while waiting for the local game processor to butcher the kill and pack our coolers. I may feel obligated to eat what I kill but I don't feel compelled to clean and dress them. So, we let a pro do that. That's what money is for. But two pigs took them a while, and we should have already been home.

Chapter Four

As we were driving home by backwoods and close enough to civilization for me to feel right about pulling out my phone. There was a raft of texts from Chloe. The first was from the day before.

Chloe: Hey! Welcome back to civilization!
   Chloe: Slay any war pigs?
   Chloe: Wait, are you still in the woods? Sorry

Then, from earlier that day:

Chloe: Back in cell range yet?
   Chloe: You are late. All, Okay?

I snorted and typed a reply.

Me: Two war pigs are slain for the good of the environment and dinner table.

Chloe: Yummy, I guess.

Me: Heavy, too.

Chloe: So, big news!

Chloe: Got invited to tag along with a crowd to Miami Beach over New Year's

Chloe: I fly back just in time for first class.

Me: I will pray for your liver.

Chloe: TY

My father just drove quietly while I went through all the texts. Then, when I set down my phone, he drawled, "Catching up with all your women?"

"Just the one," I said carefully.

"Is she holding up without your masculine presence?"

"She's fine," I said firmly, eager to assert that I was not tangled in an ever-constricting tangle. "She is going to Miami Beach at the end of Christmas break."

"Really?" my father said. "And how are you feeling about that?" he asked. "Or are you now going to leave us early to keep an eye on her?"

"No, Dad." I pondered my relationship with Chloe for the umpteenth time. "Chloe and I aren't possessive."

"Really," said my father, voice dripping with sarcasm. "So, if she hooks up with some drunken, muscle-bound Cubano in a hotel, you won't be put out?"

"No."

"Sure."

"Look," I said, "that isn't her M.O., and if she did choose to, who would I be to complain? I'm also with her... her best friend." That was close to a disastrous slip of the tongue.

My father just drove for a minute or so. "All right, that's some new information. One girl is named 'Chloe,' and the other is

Chloe's best friend."

"Quit digging, Dad!"

My father just laughed his ass off.

My phone rang when we were less than a half hour from home.

Noel.

I kept the screen turned away from Dad, but I couldn't resist answering. I wanted to hear her voice.

"Hello," I said happily, leaning away from the driver's side and pressing the phone tight to my ear.

"Hello, darling! Are you alone?" asked Noel quietly.

"Umm, no," I said. "My father and I are driving back home."

"Would you like to call me back?"

"No, I can hear you fine, thanks," I said casually, as if to a customer service agent.

"So, you are still in the car with your father? But he can't hear me?"

"That's right. It's cool."

"Tell him I said hi," Noel laughed.

"No way, man. I'm not going there," I said firmly. She laughed again.

My father, who hadn't seemed to be paying attention, leaned over slightly and asked, soft voice, "Which one is that? 'Chloe,' or the best friend?"

I glared at Dad silently.

"So you can speak freely," said Noel slowly, "but you can only listen and not reply…."

"I don't know if we have to do that," I replied slowly.

"Did you think about me at night, in the woods?" purred Noel.

Gulp. "I think we can agree on that."

Noel chuckled softly. "Which did you think about more? Our night in the hotel in the sky or the next morning?"

"I'm not sure I can say," I said neutrally but in a shallow breath.

"I bet it was the morning," she went on softly. "The morning I and that beautiful penis of yours both got up before you. The morning you woke up, you found me impaled upon you, rising and falling slowly... softly... so damned happily."

I gulped quietly, unable to trust myself to say anything.

"As your eyes opened, you lifted your hands and grasped my breasts. You did it so softly, so gentlemanly, yet so hungrily. I rose, fell atop you faster, and pressed your hands into my chest. I reveled in your amazing hardness as it drilled ecstasy into my insides, over and repeatedly. Your hips rose off the bed, pressing yourself into me even closer, all-in time with my gentle, wonderful ride."

I had to adjust the way the seat belt pulled across my lap. It was the last thing I wanted to do, with my freaking father driving right next to me, but it was non-optional.

"The sun peeked through the clouds, stabbing into our room and across the bed, just as I felt your steely rod inside me swell even more. I gasped as I felt you fill me burst after burst, and my ecstasy surged around you in return. I don't remember how long my back arched, my breasts pressing forward into your grasp. I remember collapsing atop you, taking my face in your hands, and kissing me so wonderfully that I almost came again."

There was silence on the line for a while.

"At least, that is what I'm betting you thought about," Noel went briskly as if she had just ticked off a shopping list. "Listen, I've got to go. This legal matter still won't resolve itself. Have a Merry Christmas!"

"Yeah," I croaked. "Have a Merry Christmas. I'll, um, talk to you soon!" Noel hung up.

My father had mercy on me and maintained a respectful silence... For about two-tenths of a mile. "Did you just have phone sex while sitting next to me in my truck?" the bastard asked, oh so fucking casually.

"Dad!" I practically shrieked. "What? What are you talking about?"

My father took his eyes off the road to stare at me for an uncomfortably long time as if we were two characters in front of a green screen on a TV show instead of hurtling along the real Interstate in a two-ton vehicle. Then, when he returned his eyes to the road, he said through a shit-eating grin, "Steven, I've been on the road more than half of my entire, pleased marriage. I know phone sex."

"Jesus, fuck, Dad! Too fucking much God-damned information!" I would be completely unable to look my mother in the eye when we returned home. Shit.

When my father's laughter subsided, he said more soberly. So, we need to get our stories straight... in terms of what I report to your mother."

"You said you weren't going to tell her!" I protested quickly.

"I have an assignment," he sighed. "Mom knows you are involved with someone, and I'm supposed to give her the low-down. So, what should I tell her? You have two girls sleeping with you. Then you just had phone sex in the car next to your dad. We need to get our facts straight is all I'm saying, your mom is not dumb. This will keep us out of trouble."

I sighed, too. The man was right. He usually was. "Okay," I said. "You can tell her I have a recent new girlfriend named Chloe. She is twenty-one and a Junior. I am of the firm opinion that she is attractive. But I am still skittish about how things are going, and I don't want to jinx it by talking about her with the family. That is all. No more."

Dad nodded judiciously. "Sounds good."

"It's all true," I said, "as far as it goes. That way, neither one of us gets in trouble later. And you even got all of that out of me on your own."

" I only learned their ages just now," added Dad triumphantly.

It was not lying to let him go on believing that 'age' was plural.

"Anyway," he went on. "I think that is enough for her to accept, at least for this visit home." He nodded to himself. "No need to add anything about the second girl who, from all available evidence, gives phone sex nearly as excellently as your mother."

"Dad! That's it. Let me out. I'll walk the last twenty-five miles!"

The old man laughed the rest of the way home while I tried to convince myself that the bastard hadn't deliberately scarred me mentally for life.

The headlights brushed across the house as we turned into the driveway. The dog is always the first to notice and sound the alarm that someone was there. My mother stepped out, hands on hips, with a smirk on her face.

"So, spill. I want all the dirty details."

"Oh…God…."

I turned to my father, who had some sinister grin on his face to match my mother's as he reached into his breast pocket and took out his cell phone.

My cell phone went off and I grabbed it out of my jacket and saw Noel sent a text message: One of the lawyers is going to Boise to be with family. Do you mind if I drive up with him and spend Christmas with you?

I reached over and showed Dad the text. "Tell her your parents would love to have her here."

"So, there is a girl! This we be a fun Christmas," Mom said.

THE END

Also by Carol Cassada, Tamsyn Beard, Tammy Campbell, Tammy Godfrey,

Other Anthologies from Warrioress Publishing

The Bloody Massacre

A Soul's Decay – Harper Shay

A darkness has found its way to Ash Creek, and it festers in the souls of shifters.

Sin Eaters were just a myth, an old legend that had been whispered throughout the centuries. That is until the first taint of evil had been felt in the peaceful town of Ah Creek. A corruption that had awoken a craving that couldn't be ignored.

Annihilation at Bayou Pointe – Brittany Wright

The administrator at Bayou Pointe gave Karman an offer she couldn't refuse.

With healthcare workers so few and far between, they used every tool they had to lure her to work with them: Child care, money, a vehicle, and even a house. All she had to do was show up and be their scapegoat, although that wasn't in the contract. Single mom, Karman, took the job, and from day one was put through hell. Something happened, released the beast, and Karman snapped. Now, the bullies aren't bullies anymore and are now worm food.

Ashes to Ashes – Tammy Godfrey

He emptied every glass he was given. His wife knew it was time to leave. After all, he is embarrassing when he's drunk. She wanted to drive but he said no. Was it a wrong turn of the wheel, or the wrong pedal pressed? The real question is, who was driving? It's only mattered to the one who lived, right? Wrong!

Bloody Masquerade – Brittany Wright & Dakota Cole

What happens when Penny breaks away from her confinement at the institution? She chooses to go to an event, however, this is not like any normal event. This is a masquerade ball and every choice made has consequences. Will the choices make Penny wiser, or will she suffer from an unknown fate?

Dark Cravings - Arianna Barton

The only thing better than blood is torture. When vampire Jessamine and her partners almost out vampires to society, she will have to do the unthinkable. Take down the leader of her clan, or face death. The kicker? He's her dad. Join Jessamine as she shows just how deadly a vampire can be, and why no matter how delicious your dark cravings are, they always come with strings attached.

Her Dragon Knight - Elise Whyles

To reclaim her throne she will need to trust in her dragon - to save her people she will need to claim his heart.

Rabbit – Nicole Brown

A weekend getaway turns deadly when old secrets are revealed. Brenna Larson meets the handsome Alex Jennings. But Ale has secrets he's not ready to share.

Where Dead Things Lie – E.R. Hendricks

When lust and murder meet, it turns into a devastating combination. Her past and present clash with her need to feed her insatiable desire. Trapped forever in her twisted game, where all dead things lie.

Milton Keynes UK
Ingram Content Group UK Ltd.
UKHW011116201123
432909UK00001B/4

9 798868 934735